太 白 陰 經

STRATEGIES
FOR THE
HUMAN
REALM

Crux of the T'ai-pai Yin-ching

Translated, with commentary, by

RALPH D. SAWYER

CONTENTS

PREFACE

Composed in the middle of the T'ang just about 750 CE, the *T'ai-pai Yin-ching* revitalized Chinese military science. Few works had been written since the end of the Warring States period, and none had survived the turbulence of the Wei-Chin period intact. Although Li Ch'üan, the book's author, can be said to have advanced Chinese military thought, his contributions in the crucial early chapters rarely offer the sort of insights preserved in the classic military works. Instead, they primarily provide new orientations and shifted emphases for the diverse materials that he melds and synthesizes.

Accordingly, in seeking to explicate his text in terms of traditional Chinese military history and theory, my comments have been confined to works still extant at the time of the *T'ai-pai Yin-ching*'s composition. Even though passages from the *Hundred Unorthodox Strategies* and *Hu-ch'ien Ching*, two important Sung dynasty manuals, might well have been consulted for additional insights, they have accordingly been eschewed in order to avoid contaminating the discussion with appraisals and formulations germane to a later era. Instead, because the *Art of War* fundamentally grounds the *T'ai-pai Yin-ching*, selected statements from Li Ch'üan's well-known commentary coupled with relevant assertions from other parts of the text itself are selectively employed to analyze and expand his thoughts.

This translation is intended for the broadest possible audience, readers with any interest in Chinese history, military history, strategy, or tactics rather than the few Sinologists who might peruse it. Thus, unlike my highly academic *Sun Pin Military Methods*, neither textual nor translation matters have been annotated. However, several editions, both traditional woodblock and contemporary typeset, as well as multiple commentaries and collateral texts have been consulted in order to resolve discrepancies and lacuna to the fullest extent possible.

The introduction seeks to outline the history of the text and orient the reader to the main concepts rather than exhaustively array the material. However, more detailed explanations and additional illustrative material from the military classics and other writings that Li incorporates in his text will be found in the chapter commentary. Furthermore, as the *T'ai-pai Yin-ching* is a theoretical work that largely harkens back to classic material, no attempt has been made to discuss the complexities of combat as actually practiced in the T'ang. (It might be noted that chariot-based units had been replaced by cavalry contingents.)

Although some samples from the *T'ai-pai Yin-ching*'s later sections are included in the introductory overview, only the crux of the text, the twenty-four theoretical chapters contained in the section designated as "Human Plans" plus one more, "Presenting the *Yüeh*," are included in the translation. The remaining seventy-five chapters, while constituting the greater bulk of the work, are concerned with highly disparate matters ranging from actual military equipment through sacrificial and divinatory methods. Important information about military thought and practices is interspersed, but apart from several chapters on siege issues, most of the material is highly esoteric as well as unrelated to the actual conduct of warfare and has therefore been left to others better versed in the arcane prognosticatory arts to render.

Ralph Sawyer
RalphSawyer.com
Summer 2012

A NOTE ON PRONUNCIATION

As I have repeatedly noted, neither of the two commonly employed orthographies facilitates the pronunciation of romanized Chinese characters for the uninitiated. Each system has its stumbling blocks and I cannot imagine that *qi* in pinyin is inherently more comprehensible to unpracticed readers than the older, largely discarded Wade-Giles *ch'i* for a sound similar to the initial part of "chicken" or *x* for the simple "she," although they are certainly no less comprehensible than *j* for "r" or *t* for "d" in Wade-Giles. However, as this work is intended for a broad audience, many of whom will have little experience with romanized Chinese words apart from a few occurrences in the news and my other works in which Wade-Giles has exclusively been used, the hyphenated break between syllables facilitates pronunciation; and specialists should have equal facility in either system, Wade-Giles is employed here with the exception of an idiosyncratic *yi* for "i" and the occasional, arbitrary inclusion of pinyin for important titles or terms.

As a crude guide to pronunciation, the following notes on the significant exceptions to normally expected sounds might prove useful:

t, as in *Tao*: without apostrophe, pronounced like *d* (pinyin *d*), otherwise *t*

p, as in *ping*: without apostrophe, pronounced like *b* (pinyin *b*), otherwise *p*

ch, as in *chuang*: without apostrophe, pronounced like *j* (pinyin *j* and *zh*), otherwise *ch*

hs, as in *hsi*: pronounced like English "sh" (pinyin *x*)

j, as in *jen*: pronounced like *r* (pinyin *r*)

Thus, the name of the famous Chou (or Zhou in pinyin) dynasty is pronounced as if written "jou" and sounds just like the English name "Joe."

INTRODUCTION

Little is known about Li Ch'üan (Li Quan 李筌), the author of the *T'ai-pai Yin-ching* (*Taibai Yinjing*), other than that he apparently held provincial-level military posts during the T'ang dynasty's difficult middle period and was probably active for at least twenty years (745 CE to 765 CE) late in Emperor Hsüan-tsung's reign. (The memorial that accompanied the book's submission to the emperor indicates he was serving in the moderately important post of Chieh-tu-shih for Ho-tung.) Accordingly, he must have experienced at least the initial decade of the devastating warfare that nearly sundered China during An Lu-shan's rebellion (755–786 CE) and painfully realized the dangers that ambitious commanders could pose to weak central authority.

Li's many years of martial service required that he assiduously study the classic military writings that had managed to survive the virtually unremitting conflict that marked the several centuries between the collapse of the Han and establishment of the brief-lived Sui. A few remnant sayings preserved in other texts and later compilations such as the *T'ai-p'ing Yü-lan* have been taken to imply that he may have authored additional short treatises. However, his introductory remarks strongly suggest that after years of pondering the core texts of China's military heritage and knowledgeably annotating the *Art of War* he contented himself with a single massive work, the *T'ai-pai Yin-ching*.

Li Ch'üan was not the only T'ang martial analyst whose thoughts have been transmitted to posterity. Even though almost certainly the product of extensive creative editing, no doubt because of the prominence of the discussants, the best-known work consists of a widely ranging dialogue between the great T'ang general Li Ching and T'ang T'ai-tsung, appropriately called *T'ang T'ai-tsung Li Wei-kung Wen-tui* (*Tang Taizong Li Weigong Wendui* 唐太宗李衛公問對) or *Questions and Replies between*

T'ang T'ai-tsung and Duke Li of Wei. Li Ching not only helped consolidate the T'ang's nascent power but also repelled external challenges and directed pacification campaigns against the Turks that significantly expanded its domain. T'ang T'ai-tsung, essentially the dynasty's progenitor, performed heroically in the field before becoming the second emperor.

In the last decades of the eight century, the famous *T'ung Tien* (*Tung Dian* 通典), the first of the early encyclopedia to include a significant military section, was compiled by Tu Yu (Du You), an influential scholar who also contributed a commentary to the *Art of War*. Although ostensibly devoted to governmental issues, one of the *T'ung Tien*'s nine sections consists of thirteen discrete chapters that focus on military affairs. However, rather than being original compositions, they instead reprise important passages from historical writings and the classic martial texts synthetically arrayed under various martial rubrics with Tu's insightful comments interspersed.

Finally, reacting to the carnage about him, in the first decade of the ninth century, another experienced military commander named Wang Chen composed a text based upon the *Tao Te Ching* that he hoped would provide a solution to the strife besetting the T'ang and the world at large. Titled the *Tao Te Ching Lun-ping Yao-yi* (道德經論兵要議) or *Essential Explanations of the* Tao Te Ching's *Martial Discussions*, it features a unique, often Confucian-based, expansion of the *Tao Te Ching*'s concepts and philosophy.

THE T'AI-PAI YIN-CHING

The book's name is just one of several enigmatic aspects. At first reading it would seem to mean something like the "hidden," "arcane," or "esoteric" (*yin*, dark and mysterious, as contrasted with *yang*, bright and clear) classic (*ching*), but according to the memorial that accompanied the text's submission to the emperor, dated 759 CE: "Your servant Li Ch'üan states: The *T'ai-pai Yin-ching* records campaigns and the military's employment. I have heard that *T'ai-pai* rules the military and is termed the great [commanding] general while yin affects slaying and attacks. Thus in employing the military we take our methods from them."

Although commentators over the centuries have avoided extensively discussing the title, the characters t'ai (太) and pai (白) normally mean "extreme/excessive" and "white" respectively. If literally followed this would require rendering the title something like *The Hidden Classic of Extreme Whiteness*, further compounding the mystery. However, even though Li vociferously rejects heavenly influences in several chapters, as a conjoined term t'ai-pai refers to Venus, the planet believed to govern military affairs. (In the five phase system of earth, metal, wood, fire, and water, Venus is correlated with metal and thus the west, autumn, oncoming cold, and punishments.) In addition, rather than simply entailing the usual range of connotations associated with the dynamic yin/yang dichotomy, including darkness and night, yin is sometimes said to refer to the moon itself, which, in its various phases, was traditionally thought to rule martial activities. Whether singly or in combination, Venus and the moon thus already had extensive superstitious and prognosticatory lore associated with them, not to mention arcane prohibitions and inimical indications.

The *T'ai-pai Yin-ching* contains a preface that explains his intent in creating a book fraught with potential detrimental consequences:

> In far antiquity people did not recognize their fathers and were as obtuse as infants. In the summer they nested in trees, in the winter they inhabited caves, and they roamed about with deer and wild boars. Sages spiritually interacted with the four seasons, harmonized the myriad things in the formless, and attained numinous knowledge. Thereafter, without spirituality [people] lacked the mind to perceive Heaven and Earth, without mind they lacked the means to know the tactics for victory and defeat.
>
> Above, mental techniques brought about the esteem of the Three August Ones and completed the Five Emperors. When worthy men acquire them they can become hegemons over

the four seas and kings of the Nine Provinces; when sagacious men penetrate them they can defend their borders and thwart strong enemies; but when stupid men acquire them they overturn the family's ancestral altars and bring about their clan's extinction. Thus when the *chün-tzu* acquires them he can remedy shortcomings, but when the menial man acquires them he overturns his fate.

For this reason military strategy must be kept secret and not promiscuously transmitted or the disaster will reach to a man's nine degrees of relatives. The reason that your servant has now written the *T'ai-pai Yin-ching* with its unorthodox plans and deceitful Tao and discussed mental techniques that produce disastrous cruelty is that without them the army could not be effective. I therefore stored it away in a stone room in a famous mountain but having received an imperial command indicating a desire to personally examine it, I dare risk death in forwarding it.

The first two paragraphs, which reflect concepts and language in the text itself, reveal Li's views on perspicacity and knowledge. Insofar as he deemed both essential to effectively governing and successfully undertaking martial affairs, they presumably justify his compilation of a cathartic military text. However, in raising the specter of the unorthodox in conjunction with deception, the last paragraph is somewhat misleading because the *T'ai-pai Yin-ching* rarely mentions the crucial concept of the unorthodox (*ch'i* 奇). Nevertheless, his comments on the *Art of War*'s discussion of the unorthodox show that he was conscious of its importance:

Directly opposing the enemy is orthodox, going forth on the flanks is unorthodox. Lacking unorthodox troops, no Three Armies commander has ever been able to contend for advantage.

During the Former Han dynasty, King Wu gathered his troops in preparation for invading Ta-liang. General T'ien Po-lü advised: "Since all our troops have assembled and encamped to the west, it will be difficult to gain any achievement without some unorthodox method. I would like to be assigned fifty thousand men and move upward along the Yangtze and Huai Rivers, consolidating the areas south of the Huai and in Ch'ang-sha before penetrating Wu-kuan pass, whereupon I can rejoin your majesty. This would be an unorthodox method." The king didn't heed him and was defeated by Chou Ya-fu. This then is a case of just being orthodox, of lacking the unorthodox.

If you engage in warfare without employing deception, it will be difficult to gain victory over the enemy. [As for one who sends forth the unorthodox "being as inexhaustible as Heaven and Earth"], it's a question of movement and rest. [The great rivers] penetrate and flow without being severed, the unorthodox changes like the sun and moon, the diminishment and flourishing of the four seasons, and the ceaselessness of cold and warmth. [The five notes of] *kung, shang, chia, wei, yü* furnish the eight tones, but the melodies performed from them can never be exhaustively heard. [The colors] are blue, yellow, red, white, and black. The flavors are sour, acrid, salty, sweet, and bitter, but in cooking the chef brings about the changes of the five flavors in kitchen cauldrons. Assaults, severing, cutting off, sudden strikes, and the strategic power of a myriad routes cannot be completely exhausted. The unorthodox and orthodox, relying on each other for their birth just like endless circle, cannot ever be exhausted.

Despite never exploring the unorthodox other than in explaining the *Classic of Grasping the Unorthodox* or venturing far into the realm of deceptive techniques, he still appears to have conceived the *T'ai-pai Yin-ching* as a subtle work that would discuss the fundamental yet ethereal aspects of military activities rather than ordinary tactics. In fact, the book is also known under the expanded title of *Shen-chi Chih-ti T'ai-pai Yin-ching*, the additional prefatory characters (神 機 制 敵) meaning "mysterious (or spiritual) subtle techniques for controlling the enemy."

Even though the *T'ai-pai Yin-ching* rarely refers to China's lengthy battlefield history, Li's comments further indicate that he was not only thoroughly familiar with commanders and battles, but also saw confirmation of many tactical principles and conclusions in historic outcomes. Although he never enters into extensive discussions, other than brief references to the great sages of antiquity and the dynastic founders scattered about the classic military writings, Li was the first martial analyst to effectively cite historic conflicts to exemplify concepts and illustrate tactics. He thus initiated a practice that was subsequently adopted in the *T'ung Tien* before being expanded by all the military compendia that follow.

MARTIAL HERITAGE AND SOURCES

Based upon the voluminous writings preserved in its vast military corpus, China has the longest continuous literate martial tradition of any culture, one that dates back to about 500 BCE. Accounts preserved in Shang dynasty oracle bones, Western Chou bronze inscriptions, and traditional chronicles such as the *Ch'un Ch'iu* (春 秋) and *Tso Chuan* (左 傳) indicate that rudimentary strategic concepts and basic tactical principles were being formulated nearly a millennium before the Spring and Autumn period (722–481) drew to a close. Nevertheless, the *Art of War*, a work of unquestionably mature military thought that has traditionally been attributed to Sun-tzu (Sunzi 孫 子 or 孫 武) and therefore dated to the end of the Spring and Autumn or early Warring States (403–221), remains the earliest text to have survived.

The increasingly lethal, internecine warfare that marked the Warring States period and saw Ch'in (Qin) systematically conquer the six major states that had survived the Spring and Autumn period prompted the composition of numerous political and military works. In addition to the *Art of War*, six martial texts remain from the many that apparently emerged in the turbulence: the *Ssu-ma Fa* (*Sima Fa* 司 馬 法), *Wu-tzu* (*Wuzi* 吳 子), *Sun Pin Ping-fa* (*Sun Bin Bingfa* 孫 臏 兵 發), *T'ai Kung Liu-t'ao* (*Tai*

Gong Liutao 太 公 六 韜), *Wei Liao-tzu* (*Wei Liaozi* 尉 繚 子), and *Huang-shih Kung San-lüeh* (*Huangshi Gong Sanlüe* 黃 石 公 三 略). (In my translations the *Sun Pin Ping-fa* is titled *Sun Pin Military Methods*, the *Liu-t'ao* the *Six Secret Teachings*, and the *Huang-shih Kung San-lüeh* the *Three Strategies of Huang-shih Kung*.)

The *Art of War* probably attained its current form about the start of the Warring States period after having been compiled within a school of military thought presumably initiated by Sun-tzu himself. (Whether the pronouncements actually originated with Sun-tzu remains a much debated issue, but for convenience our commentary will continue to refer to him as if he is the work's progenitor.) The *Wu-tzu* probably followed within a century, especially if any of the text can actually be identified with the exemplary commander Wu Ch'i. The famed strategist Sun Pin flourished in the middle of the fourth century and his compilation, an updated but highly creative derivative of the *Art of War*, attained its final form by the end of the century. Next came the *Liu-t'ao* (*Six Secret Teachings*) nominally attributed to the famous early Western Chou (Zhou) strategist known as the T'ai Kung but definitely a compilation of the middle to late Warring States, and finally the *Wei Liao-tzu* at the end of that era. The date of the *Three Strategies* remains controversial, but it probably was composed about the same time as the *Wei Liao-tzu* or possibly the very early Former Han. Only the often laconic *Ssu-ma Fa* remains truly puzzling. Although it purportedly preserves Western Chou military thought and sometimes seems archaic, it includes many passages similar in style and content to other late Warring States contemplations, both military and political.

Together with the *Military Methods*, a treatise that had been lost by the T'ang but retained a shadowy existence through scattered pronouncements embedded in other books, these works comprise what might conveniently be termed the classic military writings. (The work presently known as the *Sun Pin Ping-fa* was laboriously reconstructed from bamboo strips preserved in a Former Han tomb excavated some four decades ago.) In 1080 CE, under imperial auspices, the six (apart from the *Military Methods*) were combined with the *Questions and Replies between T'ang T'ai-tsung and Duke Li of Wei* to produce the now famous Sung dynasty military compendium known as the *Wu-ching Ch'i-shu* (武 經 七 書) or *Seven Military Classics*.

Living in the middle of the T'ang dynasty, Li Ch'üan would have also had access to a variety of early philosophical writings including the *Shang-chün Shu* (*Shangjun Shu* 商 軍 書), *Meng-tzu* (*Mengzi* 孟 子, known in translation as the *Mencius*), *Hsün-tzu* (*Xunzi* 荀 子), *Huai-nan Tzu* (*Huainan Zi* 淮 南 子), and even the *Mo-tzu* (*Mozi* 墨 子). Their authors all pondered military affairs, and several of the nonmilitary books contain chapters dedicated to martial expositions as well as to decrying the horrendous consequences of conflict. Furthermore, the *Mo-tzu* is particularly famed for its explanation of siege practices, while Mencius's discussions of Virtue and kingly government would subsequently furnish a basis for moralizing whenever imperial debates about the feasibility of mounting aggressive campaigns against external peoples arose.

Hsün-tzu (Xunzi 荀 子) is noted as a political thinker of the middle Warring States period whose reinterpretation of Confucius's teachings made them both more realistic and relevant to the administrative needs of the state. Many *T'ai-pai Yin-ching* passages either directly reflect his conceptions or naturally harmonize with them, including that heaven proceeds in an orderly, naturalistic way and that good government based upon laws and pervasively accepted forms of civilization is essential. Thus, in "Troops" Li states that "states must establish the customary forms of behavior (*li*), fidelity, intimacy, and love before men will exchange hunger for surfeit. The customs of filiality, loving-kindness, integrity, and shame must prevail in the state before men exchange death for life." According to Hsün-tzu, only prosperous, well-regulated, and militarily powerful states possess the awesomeness needed to deter attacks and remain aloof from entanglements.

Li similarly had a thorough knowledge of numerous historical texts including the *Tso Chuan*, *Chou Li* (周 禮), *Shih Chi* (史 記), *Wu Yüeh Ch'un-ch'iu* (吳 越 春 秋), and especially the *Tao Te Ching* (道 德 經), philosophic Taoism's foundation, a work that had been compiled from disparate materials by the middle of the Warring

States period and will be cited in my commentary to several chapters. The *Huai-nan Tzu*, traditionally identified with Taoism but a much more eclectic and discursive effort than the *Tao Te Ching*, similarly pondered a wide range of fundamental issues ranging from Heaven, Earth, and Man to life's ideal form and numerous transcendental and esoteric issues. Numerous implications are drawn for the human realm, and the *Huai-nan Tzu* even includes a chapter dedicated to discussing military affairs. Not just the contents but also the language of the *T'ai-pai Yin-ching* betrays considerable familiarity with the work and a thoroughgoing acceptance of many of its doctrines.

In the *T'ai-pai Yin-ching*, Li also mentions a shadowy figure known as Kuei-ku Tzu (鬼 谷 子) or the Master of Ghost Valley, who is thought to have been a mountain-dwelling recluse. His insights into human affairs and strategy were supposedly appropriated by several famous figures who then dramatically affected Warring States history. His reputed disciples included Sun Pin and Li Ssu, as well as Chang Yi and Su Ch'in, two itinerant persuaders who sought to influence the formation and dissolution of the crucial horizontal and vertical alliances. Whether this elusive sage ever existed remains unknown, but the reverence he continues to be accorded and the numerous, often massive secondary works devoted to explicating his thoughts well reflect the traditional Chinese emphasis upon winning through wisdom rather than combat and force. (With few exceptions, throughout Chinese history the reality would generally be otherwise as states engaged in a quest to annihilate each other, resulting in the populace being nearly exterminated in recurrent episodes of total warfare.)

The *T'ai-pai Yin-ching* shows great familiarity with the contents of the work identified with him, appropriately called the *Kuei-ku Tzu*. An esoteric yet eclectic work very much in the tradition of the *Tao Te Ching* and *Huai-nan Tzu*, the *Kuei-ku Tzu* has multiple foci but is primarily concerned with the three realms of Heaven, Earth, and Man, governing through wisdom in an essentially actionless way, and understanding men and employing them. Li Ch'üan obviously found the book's approach to conceptualizing the universe and charting human activities appealing because he frequently employs concepts, images, and language from the highly laconic and sometimes enigmatic pronouncements. However, whether Kuei-ku Tzu actually composed the text known to have existed in the Sui and T'ang in the Warring States period or it was a later forgery remains uncertain.

Li Ch'üan's treatise often appears to be just a pastiche of important passages from these writings, particularly the *Art of War*, with certain connectives added. Although a somewhat misleading impression, because the times had changed and he has reoriented the material as well as subsumed it within a revised conceptual framework, the *T'ai-pai Yin-ching* incontestably consists primarily of materials drawn from earlier eras.

Unfortunately, with the exception of the first chapter, Li never indicates his sources or even whether he is adapting ancient concepts and theories. Much of the content is immediately recognizable to anyone thoroughly familiar with the classic military texts, but he complicates the task by resorting to other Warring States political thinkers such as Shang Yang. Moreover, in many cases he paraphrases, simply summarizes the essential meaning, or quotes from memory, thereby distorting the originals sufficiently to prevent their identification with any degree of confidence. Moreover, it should be remembered that Li was writing about what interested him rather than necessarily building a comprehensive edifice from materials of identical neutrality.

Concepts and principles from the *Art of War* invariably take precedence not just because Sun-tzu's short treatise was and still, in many ways, remains the foundation of Chinese military science, but also because Li commented extensively on it, reviving a tradition that seems to have been somewhat neglected since Ts'ao Ts'ao's efforts at the end of the Later Han. (Their notations are preserved in the famous Sung dynasty *Ten Commentaries* [*Shih-chia Chu*] edition.) However, even though the *Art of War* begins with the historically famous statement, "Warfare is the great affair of state, the basis of life and death, the Tao to survival or extinction," Li surprisingly never cites it in the *T'ai-pai Yin-ching* despite being totally in agreement with the immediate conclusion that "it must be thoroughly pondered and analyzed." (His commentary indicates that he interpreted the first character, *ping* 兵 in 兵 者 國 之 大 事 as "weapons" rather than the "military," its more extended meaning, for he states that "weapons are baleful implements. Life and death, existence and perishing are bound up with them. For this reason Sun-tzu emphasizes them, fearing that men will lightly employ them.")

Although heavily based upon the *Art of War*, the *T'ai-pai Yin-ching* is far more than a collection of *Art of War* materials cobbled together with statements abstracted from his previous commentary. Instead, within the context of wisdom and Virtue, Li selectively adopts, intermixes, and synthesizes focal concepts integral to the organization and practice of warfare from the *Tao Te Ching*, *Wei Liao-tzu*, *Three Strategies*, *Hsün-tzu*, *Huai-nan Tzu*, and Shang Yang's *Shang-chün Shu* as well as the *Six Secret Teachings*. (Complete sections from the latter appear in chapters such as "Techniques Include Clandestine Plans.") Appropriately, many of his passages, even entire chapters, would subsequently be incorporated virtually unaltered into the compendia compiled over the next thousand years.

Moreover, while he never explicitly denies the validity of Sun-tzu's concepts or tactical principles, his comments to several *Art of War* passages show that he was not reluctant to reinterpret implications or modify possible conclusions. For example, in "Configurations of Terrain," Sun-tzu states that "if, when their strategic power is equal, one attacks ten, this is called 'running off.'" Li's annotation states, "They did not calculate their strength. If you gain terrain with an advantageous configuration and employ the strategy of unorthodox ambushes, it would be possible."

FUNDAMENTAL CONCEPTS

Although tactics are surprisingly absent and the *T'ai-pai Yin-ching* lacks the comprehensiveness of the *Six Secret Teachings*, its one hundred often compact chapters constitute a veritable repository of T'ang military theory and specialized practices. Much in accord with prevailing cosmological concepts, the book opens with a disquisition on Heaven and Earth but asserts that human effort alone determines the outcome of battles and fate of states. Having established the realm of discussion, Li then proceeds to the crux of his vision, outlining the methods and approach required by the inimical changes experienced since the legendary Sages created civilization and imposed order.

Foremost is the realization that wisdom, preferably as manifest by Sages, and talent provide the foundation of effective government and thus the very possibility of undertaking externally directed martial activities. By rejecting aggressive warfare motivated by anger, a quest for fame, or territorial acquisition, the *Art of War* had transformed warfare from being an emotional or extemporaneous activity into a constrained, rational undertaking. Sun-tzu had therefore emphasized the need for military intelligence, calculation, and net assessments to determine the likelihood of victory. In accord with might be said to have been his vision of efficient warfare, the objective should not be simply achieving a hundred victories in a hundred clashes but conquering without combat. This can only be accomplished through such thorough knowledge that the enemy's alliances can be destroyed and their plans balked.

Li Ch'üan not only embraced Sun-tzu's concept but also expanded the means to include the sort of subversive measures systematically practiced in the late Spring and Autumn period and advocated, as well as detailed, in the *Six Secret Teachings*. As he noted in his memorial, these methods are inherently perverse, but without them the state cannot expect to survive in an environment of disparaged ethical values marked by the brutal exercise of power. Of course, just as Sun-tzu asserted would be required to effectively employ clandestine agents, their implementation must be tempered by sagacity and righteousness and then undertaken only by men of Virtue.

All the crucial concepts initially articulated by the *Art of War*, including strategic power (*shih* 勢), the tactical imbalance of power (*ch'üan* 權), the advantages of intelligently exploiting specific configurations of terrain (*ti-hsing* 地形), and the importance of manipulating the enemy, appear as core elements in the *T'ai-pai Yin-ching*. Enticements, deception, and misinformation provide the basic means for manipulating the enemy, but being formless and unknowable realizes the pinnacle of befuddling and incapacitating opponents. In a swirling, unstable context, everyone entrusted with responsibility, whether civil officials or military commanders, must therefore be astute men of character rather than self-serving minions or benighted bravados. They must be carefully evaluated through situational tests and subjected to rigorous questioning intended to confound them into revealing their real personalities, capabilities, and intentions.

Issues of command and control naturally arise in this connection. Apart from pondering the essence of exemplary leadership and the problems raised in the *Art of War*, Li also assigns a formative role to the time-honored measures of rewards and punishments, otherwise known as the twin handles of power. However, more than most writers (and contrary to Shang Yang), Li Ch'üan was aware of the need not just for adequate material resources but also a burgeoning economy that equally combined commerce with agriculture. Thereafter, harmonizing the people in the Tao and uniting them in their commitment to the state's enterprises under a vigorous but ever virtuous national leadership would be paramount, with neither the civil nor martial being neglected. Only then might a well-disciplined, highly motivated army under knowledgeable commanders take the field confident of success. Naturally, all activity must be timely—a concept not specifically explored in the *Art of War*—and opportunities fervently exploited.

LATER CHAPTERS

The first twenty-four chapters of the book, the crux of the conceptual and theoretical work, although ostensibly focused on "human plans" (*jen-mou* 人 謀) or affairs, actually encompass the greater issues of strategic concepts, command, and operations. Thereafter the *Tai-pai Yin-ching* turns to the more diverse material initiated by a section titled "Tsa-yi Lei" (雜 儀 類) or "Miscellaneous Discussions" that encompasses matters concerned with military leadership ranging from ritually appointing the chief general through questions of hierarchy and the sort of offenses for which severe punishments must be imposed. The section also includes two chapters - - "Scrutinizing Men" and "Appraising Horses" - - devoted to evaluating men for command and horses for military service. Both of them are surprisingly based upon external appearance rather than inner character or personality traits and thus reflect beliefs associated with the burgeoning practice of physiognomy rather than the methods of active evaluation seen in "Techniques for Probing the Mind" and "Mirroring Talent."

"Scrutinizing Men" (or "Mirroring Men" 鑒 人) actually begins with a strikingly clear assertion of transparency:

> Observing a man's exterior is sufficient to know his interior. The seven orifices of the head are the gates and doors to the five viscera. All the aspects of the head and the prominence of the forehead, nose, and chin define the face's features. The appearance of wisdom or stupidity, courage or fear is expressed by a single inch of eyes. From the indications of Heaven and markings of wealth, they are separated into noble and ignoble, poor and rich. Now, if you want to entrust a general with command, first observe his facial appearance and afterward know his mind.

Many of the descriptions are remarkably precise, allowing immediately differentiating men in terms of potential and individual category, but others are quite imaginative and nebulous, of little immediate utility. Among the more cohesive are the descriptions of energetic, fat, and benevolent people:

> Indications of an abundance of spirit: their facial expressions are grave and dignified; they are marked by integrity and energy; their intentions are unaffected by the pleasures of music or the allure of sex; and their principles of

self-cultivation are unchanged by prosperity or adversity. This is termed an abundance of spirit.

Indications of a corpuscular abundance: the tops of their heads are abundant and broad; their bellies thick; noses straight but rounded at the end; mouths square and protruding; and chins and foreheads closing toward each other. They have high cheekbones and ears; excessively corpulent coarse bones that however are not visible; eyebrows and eyes that are bright and clear; and fresh red hands and feet. When they look down on inferiors, they seem tall, but compared to the great they are solitary and small. This is termed an abundance of physique.

Indications of an abundance of heart: they conceal the evil in others and raise their good points; put themselves last and others first; do not deprecate others in order to make themselves seem worthy, nor do they endanger other men to make themselves secure. They perform unseen acts of Virtue; always preserve loyalty and sincerity; are liberal and magnanimous; and are unconcerned by petty morality. This is an abundance of heart.

"Shou Yüeh" or "Bestowing the *Yüeh* [Ax of Command]," the first chapter in the section and twenty-fifth in the entire *Tai-pai Yin-ching*, describes a ceremony that Li believed should be employed for appointing the commanding general. (A virtually identical ceremony preserved in the *Six Secret Teachings* no doubt provided the basis for Li's redaction.) Brief but still highly ritualized, it was intended to enhance the leader's awesomeness in accord with Li Ch'üan's emphasis upon his importance to the state as seen in the book's earlier chapters and described in the following chapter, "Chiang Chün" (蔣 軍), or "The General," rather than just formally transfer temporal battlefield authority. "The General" then commences by stating that "the masses of the Three Armies, the command of a myriad men, the weighing and establishing of lightness and heaviness, all lie with one man. He must be investigated. A single man is appointed as commanding general who must be wise, trustworthy, benevolent, courageous, strict, cautious, worthy, and enlightened." The chapter titled "Ch'en Chiang" ("Formation Generals" 陳 將) continues Li's discussion of generals by offering several interesting observations on the nature of power and authority while as usual emphasizing distinction and wisdom:

> People with similar wisdom cannot employ each other, people with equal strength cannot defeat each other, and people with the same authority cannot govern each other. Those whose Tao is the same cannot rule each other, whose power is the same cannot be kings over each other, whose emotions are the same cannot accord with each other. When emotions differ they can be governed, when the same they lead to chaos. Thus the commanding general [leads] with wisdom, lieutenant commanders with courage. When the wise lead the courageous what cannot be accomplished?

"Tui Chiang" ("Section Generals" 隊 將), another of the chapters focused on command, essentially replicates material from the *Art of War* also found in the *T'ai-pai Yin-ching*'s earlier chapters:

> The classics state that when the wise employ the stupid, they cause their ears to be deaf and their eyes to be blind and mystify their hearts (minds) for only thereafter will they heed their commands. It might be compared to racing a herd of sheep, they race them forward, race them back, but no one knows where. It is like climbing up high and kicking aside the ladder. When one enters the borders of the feudal lords, discard the bridges. Labor them with affairs, do not inform them of the plans. Speak to them about the profits, do not tell them about the harm. Then the officers can gain their hearts and the ruler their bodies. In this way when death and life, assembling and dispersing are decided by one, he is termed a good general.

Having completed his scrutiny of command issues, Li Ch'üan proceeds to examine the equipment used in the conduct of warfare, regulations for encamping and related issues, and the nature of formations and deployments in "Chan-chü-lei" (戰 具 類) before veering into the more esoteric subjects of sacrificial observances and prognostication. Although incendiary warfare had been increasingly employed in the preceding centuries and its methods were multiplying, the *T'ai-pai Yin-ching* was the first text since the *Mo-tzu* to describe any of the techniques and depict actual delivery devices for both incendiary and, to a lesser extent, aquatic warfare. Thereafter, most of the later military manuals and compendia simply adopted these chapters when undertaking discussions of these two subjects. (An overview may be found in my *Fire and Water: The Art of Incendiary and Aquatic Warfare in China*.)

In "Huo-kung-chü" ("Equipment for Incendiary Attacks" 火 攻 具) Li briefly outlines the essentials in a passage that draws upon the *Art of War*'s infamous chapter "Incendiary Attacks": "The [*Art of War*] states that 'using fire to aid an attack is enlightened.' When the weather is dry and parched; the encampment's huts are fashioned from reeds or bamboo; or they have piled hay, grain, and the army's provisions among dry grass or withered undergrowth, and the moon is in the lodges of *chi, pi, yi,* or *chen* at dusk, prepare equipment for the five incendiary attacks, exploit the south wind, and burn them."

The chapter titled "Kung-ch'eng-chü" ("Equipment for Attacking Cities" 攻 城 具) outlines a multistage incendiary technique that disperses a flammable medium with the first volley, ignites the fires with the second, and ensures a conflagration by adding readily combustible fuel: "Take small gourds full of oil, affix them to the tips of arrows, and shoot them onto the roofs of towers and turrets. After the gourds break and the oil disperses, use flaming arrows to hit the dispersed oil. As soon as fires are ignited, continue shooting gourds of oil. The towers and turrets will be completely incinerated."

According to "Huo Shih" ("Fire Arrows" 火 矢), a somewhat simpler method is employed for attacking flammable materials stored within enemy encampments: "Select archers capable of shooting three hundred paces and cap the ends of arrows with gourds filled with fire. Employ several hundred of them, waiting until the middle of the night to shoot them en masse into the enemy's encampment to burn their stores and provisions. When fires arise and their army is in chaos, exploit the opportunity to fervently attack."

Turning to tactics, although "Huo Tao" ("Incendiary Thief" 火 盗) describes a clandestine arsonist, Li outlines another approach to effecting an incendiary attack in "Huo Ping" ("Incendiary Troops" 火 兵): "At night, employ elite cavalry with gags and tie up the horses' mouths. Each man should carry a bundle of faggots, straw, and grass on his back together with a container of burning embers and proceed directly to the enemy's encampment. They should set their fires all at once. If the encampment is startled and chaotic, urgently exploit it. If it remains quiet and ordered, abandon the effort."

The possibility that enraged animals could be employed as unstoppable vehicles for spreading fire and disrupting the enemy had become evident when T'ien Tan famously exploited a large number of "fire oxen" to successfully break out of Chi-mo after a multiyear siege. Cognizant of this incident, Li expanded the technique in "Huo Shou" ("Incendiary Animals" 火 獸), "Huo Ch'in" ("Fire Birds" 火 禽), and "Kung-ch'eng Chü" ("Equipment for Attacking Cities") by developing triggering methods suited to a variety of animals, including pigs and birds:

Stuff burning moxa into gourds, make four holes, then tie them to the necks of a wild pig or deer. Singe their tails and release them toward the enemy's encampment, causing them to race into the grass there. When the gourds break, fires will start.

Empty out a walnut and make two holes in it. Fill it with burning moxa and tie it to the foot of a wild chicken. Prick its tail and release it so that when it flies into the grass and the walnut splits open, fires will start.

Hollow out an apricot (core), stuff it with burning moxa, and tie it to the feet of a bird. Toward dusk, release a flock of them so that they will fly into the city to roost for the night. Fires will shortly break out in the huts where they congregate.

A corresponding chapter dedicated to protection—"Shou-ch'en-chü" ("Incendiary Devices in Defense" 守 城 具)—reveals that incendiary measures had already acquired an integrated role in defense: iron chains used to lower pine torches down outside the city walls in order to illuminate the base area; "swallow tail torches," a kind of torch with the ends split so that they would hold while burning after being dropped onto the peaks of mobile protective roofing; oil sacks that could be thrown down; and "traveling fire" that contrary to its name did not move about freely but was contained in a swinging iron basket hung over the side of the walls. Additionally, another section, "Sou-shan Shao-ts'ao" ("Search the Mountains and Burn the Grass" 搜 山 燒 草), advised implementing an even more basic preventive measure: "On the first day of the tenth month, burn the grass around strategic points and routes, as well as about the city, to prevent concealment and being employed against you."

The next section ("Yü-pei" 預 備) includes numerous chapters on preparations and encampments, a brief discussion of logistics and provisions, and two chapters already mentioned, "Sou-shan Shao-ts'ao" and "Kung-ch'eng Chü." Thereafter, Li proceeds to the critical issue of formations and deployments in "Ch'en-t'u" (陳 圖), a portion of the text that merits a separate study because it includes a number of highly detailed chapters of considerable historical importance in which diagrams and figures are often provided. Furthermore, in view of his apparent assignment of a critical role to the unorthodox, his comments in "Ho-erh-wei-yi Chen-t'u" ("Diagram of Deployments for Uniting to Make One" 合 而 為 一 陳 圖) are particularly germane to contemplating the *T'ai-pai Yin-ching*'s contents:

One who excels at warfare engages with the orthodox and wrests victory with the unorthodox. The mutual production of the unorthodox and orthodox is just like an endless cycle.

Who can exhaust them? The unorthodox is yang, the orthodox is yin. When yin and yang intermix, the four seasons proceed.

The unorthodox is the firm, the orthodox is the flexible. When the firm and flexible gain each other, the myriad things are completed amidst them. Through employing the unorthodox and orthodox the myriad things are all conquered. What is referred to as "joining" is the joining of the eight unorthodox and orthodox formations to be one.

Surprisingly, contrary to common views that regard normal tactical efforts as yang and irregular ones as yin, this passage identifies the unorthodox as yang and the orthodox as yin. Accordingly, the unorthodox is also viewed as being "firm" and the orthodox as "flexible," again contrary to normal expectation and fraught with implications that deserve to be explored.

The seventh section undertakes the discussion of three distinct subjects: sacrificial rites for such legendary martial figures as Ch'ih Yu, reporting victory or defeat, and medicinal prescriptions. However, it is with the eighth that a major disjuncture occurs because it and the remaining two sections are devoted to divinatory and prognosticatory methods, calendrical indications for auspicious days, and determining the proper geospatial orientation before engaging in battle. Many of the processes intended to designate promising circumstances are quite intricate and complex. Therefore, whether T'ang dynasty commanders ever followed them or other prognosticatory indications in the quest to achieve a hundred victories in a hundred encounters remains an open question.

Somewhat more mystifying is the origin of these traditional materials and Li Ch'üan's purpose in surprisingly incorporating them because the *T'ai-pai Yin-ching* begins by embracing Sun-tzu's stress on human agency and rejecting the influence of Heaven. They may well be an accretion of later centuries, simply cobbled together with the more mundane material because of the book's appealingly esoteric title. Nevertheless, their inclusion does not seem completely discordant because Li does speak of yin and yang, Heaven and Earth in the earlier chapters. Moreover, having originated in the Shang and continued throughout the ensuing twenty-five hundred years despite sometimes being vehemently rejected, martial divinatory materials not only had a long tradition but had also continued to proliferate, with increasingly large amounts being incorporated in the later military compendia, including the *Hu-ch'ien Ching*. Unfortunately, resolution of this conundrum must await dedicated studies by those with greater expertise.

Nevertheless, in his commentary to "Vacuity and Substance," Li notes that forthcoming activity ("movement and rest") can be known by observing cloud *ch'i* above the enemy. This is not too dissimilar from the thrust of two *Six Secret Teachings* chapters, "The Five Notes" and "The Army's Indications," because the latter concludes that the *ch'i* over a city will indicate whether it can be attacked, the inhabitants suffer from illness, or the defenders will mount a resilient defense. Li offers two examples in his commentary, the first from a battle that proved pivotal in the quest to displace the usurper Wang Mang in the interstice between the Former and Later Han dynasties: "During Wang Mang's era, Wang Hsün was conducting a punitive campaign against K'un-yang. The cloud *ch'i* above their encampment dropped down like a ruined mountain, suddenly disappearing only a few feet away. [The future emperor] Kuang Wu knew that Wang would certainly be defeated."

The basic theory of *ch'i* / cloud prognostication is outlined in "Chan Yün Ch'i" ("Fathoming Cloud *Ch'i*" 占 雲 氣): "When Heaven and Earth mutually respond, yin and yang mutually interact, it is termed *ch'i*. When *ch'i* accumulates over a long time, it becomes clouds. In all cases things attain form below, and *ch'i* responds above. Thus it is said, 'By fathoming the *ch'i* one will know affairs, by looking at the *ch'i* know people.'" As might be expected, these manifestations apply symmetrically. Therefore, any indications detectable above your own encampment should equally provide actualizable information.

The *ch'i* manifestations included in the *T'ai-pai Yin-ching* range from simple phenomena that can be correlated with imminent consequences (such as a reddish diffusion in the sky presaging great bloodshed) through highly imaginative configurations including dragons cavorting and headless men. "Meng Chiang Ch'i" ("*Ch'i* of Fierce Generals" 猛 將 氣) introduces the process by stating that "when a fierce general is about to move, his *ch'i* will first be manifest." For example, "A fierce general's *ch'i* is like a dragon or tiger in the mood for killing. A fierce general's *ch'i* is like smoke and fog, fulminating up like the light from a fire illuminating the night. A fierce general's location will have reddish white *ch'i* surrounding it."

Ch'i manifestations were even believed to provide an indication of character and otherwise reveal information about the army: "If the *ch'i* above the enemy's encampment is yellow white and glistening, the general has awesome virtue and cannot be attacked. If the *ch'i* is greenish white and high, the general is very courageous. If before a great battle it is white and low to the front but green and high to the rear, the general is afraid but the officers courageous. If it's voluminous to the front but patchy to the rear, the lieutenant generals are afraid and unenlightened."

Among the "intelligence" that might be gleaned was the existence of secret plots. Thus "Meng Chiang Ch'i" notes that "if the *ch'i* above the enemy's army gradually assumes a form like a mountain in the clouds, the general has secret plots and cannot be attacked." Accordingly, the *T'ai-pai Yin-ching* contains a brief chapter focusing on *ch'i* phenomena that warn of subversive activities, "Yin-mou Ch'i" ("*Ch'i* of Secret Plots" 陰 謀 氣). Illuminating manifestations include "If black *ch'i* approaches your army like a chariot wheel turning, the enemy is plotting to stir up chaos and conspiring with minor ministers from your state, so you should investigate it" and "If the sky is sunk in darkness without any rain so that during the day the sun is not visible nor the stars or moon at night for more than three days, there is a secret plot. The commanding general should take precautions against his attendants."

Sun-tzu's *Art of War* concludes by sighting the exemplary roles played by Yi Yin and the T'ai Kung in overthrowing the Hsia and Shang respectively. Li Ch'üan's comment—"In discussing the military, Sun-tzu begins with assessment and ends with agents, so he probably did not take attacking to be the main subject. Can anyone who fulfills the role of a general not be cautious about this!" — perhaps explains the thrust of the *T'ai-pai Yin-ching*, realizing victory whenever possible without engaging in combat. Although the prognosticatory materials stem from another tradition, he may have felt they would prompt a calculated examination of the situation even if the information they provided, while appearing concrete and detailed, was actually quite nebulous.

人謀

JEN MOU STRATEGIES FOR THE HUMAN REALM

1

天 無 陰 陽

"HEAVEN LACKS YIN AND YANG"

A classic states that "Heaven's roundness and earth's squareness have their basis in yin and yang. Once yin and yang have attained form, contravening them will result in defeat, according with them will result in success." This probably refers to carefully sustaining the agricultural seasons, not to employing the military.

Heaven and Earth do not exist for [the sake of] the ten thousand things, the myriad things exist through relying upon Heaven and Earth. Yin and yang were not born for the sake of the myriad things, the myriad things are given birth through relying upon yin and yang. [As the *Tao Te Ching* states], "Heaven and Earth are not benevolent but treat the myriad things like straw dogs." What compassion do yin and yang have for the myriad things?

Now, fire's inherent nature is to be hot, it is not scorching and burning the myriad things that produces its hotness. Water's inherent nature is to be wet, it does not give birth to moisture

3

in order to float and convey the myriad things. Water and fire are singular in their nature, but the manner in which the myriad things encounter them differs. Yin and yang are singular in nature, but the manner in which the myriad things encounter them varies from burgeoning through withered. If water and fire had compassion, they could float stones and submerge trees, liquefy metals and solidify earth. But [as they cannot], it is clear that yin and yang are not able to produce victory or defeat, ensure survival or bring about extinction, indicate auspiciousness or balefulness, goodness and evil.

When the spring winds blow from the east, grass and tree kernels split open, yet the grain in storehouses does not sprout. In autumn cold vapors slay the hundred flowering plants, and they all wither, but the grass stored away is not harmed. Yin and yang, cold and heat can be changed by human plans, so how can the success or defeat of human plans be affected by yin and yang?

In antiquity [the usurper] Wang Mang summoned everyone who excelled in secret plans and entrapping methods, some sixty-three in all, and fully prepared his army and officers. But when he was defeated at K'un-yang, it happened that a thunderstorm arose that was so severe that roofing tiles blew off and rain poured down. At this moment had the *san men* (three auspicious gates) not been strictly [guarded] nor generals for the five [prominent] directions not all present? Mistakenly trusting in the computations of *Chi-men Tun-chia* methodology, the indications provided by the movements of *T'ai-sui*, and the zodiac's monthly establishment resulted in this disaster!

In olden times there was Chang Po-sung, who fled turbulent times and dwelled in a military encampment. Hard pressed by the brigands, the stalwart warriors all fled. However, Po-sung said, "Today the [sun's indications] are discordant, so we cannot go out and rush off." Shortly thereafter the brigands arrived, Po-sung was slain, his wife and children became prisoners, and all his wealth was stolen. Huan T'an said in his *Hsin Lun* that "even the stupidest people know to avoid evil times. What use are yin and yang to people who do not avoid inimical affairs?"

4

The T'ai Kung said: "If you entrust matters to the worthy and employ the capable, affairs will be advantageous even without conducive times; if you are enlightened about laws and scrutinize ordinances, affairs will be auspicious without conducting divination and prognostication; if you honor achievement and reward effort, even without conducting expiatory rituals you will be blessed." Lacking generous Virtue and true enlightenment yet relying on the calculations of the sun and moon; failing to recognize (assess) the enemy's strengths and weaknesses yet trusting to the luck of Heavenly times; bereft of wisdom and plans but looking to [the indications of] cloud *ch'i*; having little courage and only minimal strength yet hoping for Heavenly blessings; being so fearful that you cannot attack but relying on divination by turtles and stalks; having officers and troops that are not courageous but relying upon ghosts and spirits; and being clumsy in setting up ambushes yet relying on [esoteric indications of] "toward" and "away" [are all examples of misguided actions].

In the Tao of Heaven, ghosts and spirits can be looked at but not seen, can be listened for but not heard, sought but not obtained. Scrutinizing these vacuous and empty indications cannot be employed to decide victory or defeat, cannot be used to control life and death. Thus enlightened generals do not model on these, but ordinary generals cannot help themselves.

Sun-tzu said: "The means by which enlightened rulers and sagacious generals moved and conquered others, that their achievements surpassed the masses, was advance knowledge. Advance knowledge cannot be gained from ghosts and spirits, inferred from phenomena, or projected from the measures of Heaven but must be sought from men." Wu-tzu said, "Assessing the enemy and committing to battle without conducting divination is based upon advance knowledge." Fan Li said, "If Heavenly seasons [*shih*] do not arise, they cannot be forced; if human affairs do not develop, they cannot be created."

Probably the "seasons of Heaven" refer to enemy states suffering harm from disasters such as floods or drought, insects or parasites, frost and hail, desiccation or chaos, not the moments of Heaven as defined by orphaned or vacuous star sites, toward or contrary

5

[motion]. The T'ai Kung said, "Sages are given birth to rectify later ages. Therefore they produced deceptive books and [writings] on achieving unorthodox victories. However, the Tao of Heaven is of no advantage to the military." If this is true, then in the Tao of Heaven what influence can yin and yang have on the military?

SAWYER

The book begins with a consideration of Heaven and its role — or rather, nonrole — in human affairs. According to "Initial Estimations" in the *Art of War*, "Heaven encompasses yin and yang, cold and heat, and the constraints of the seasons." No doubt because they had become a matter of unshakable belief since emerging as fundamental concepts in the quest to understand the universe during the Warring States period, Li does not deny the existence of yin and yang. Instead, much as Hsün-tzu, he posits them as indifferent to human activity and forcefully asserts that efforts to derive useful indications from Heavenly phenomena are not just futile but fundamentally inapplicable.

The theocratic Shang dynasty that preceded the Chou (Zhou) had employed divination by turtle plastrons and oxen scapula to determine the auspiciousness of contemplated activities, including military campaigns, the selection of commanders, and various tactics that might be employed. Although the Chou was familiar with Shang methods, another divinatory system, now known from its embodiment as the *Yi Ching* (or *Book of Change*), based upon casting milfoil stalks and evaluating the resulting pattern of six yin and yang lines evolved during the Western Chou. It was similarly employed in martial contexts to evaluate the enemy and determine the feasibility of proposed military actions in the Spring and Autumn period. Remarkably, Sun-tzu rejected this highly entrenched heritage and instead boldly asserted that only information acquired through human agency could have any validity, thereby justifying the extensive employment of the sort of clandestine agents discussed in his infamous chapter "Employing Agents" and in the *T'ai-pai Yin-ching*'s "Roving Agents."

Other political and martial thinkers subsequently reasserted the irrelevance of divinatory and other mantic methods, including the author of the *Wei Liao-tzu*, a work compiled late in the Warring States period. According to the argument found in "Heavenly Offices":

> King Hui of Liang inquired of Wei Liao-tzu: "Is it true that through punishments and Virtue the Yellow Emperor achieved a hundred victories [without ever suffering a defeat]?"
>
> Wei Liao-tzu replied: "Punishment was employed to attack [the rebellious], Virtue was employed to preserve [the people]. This is not what is referred to as 'Heavenly Offices,' '[auspicious] hours and days,' 'yin and yang,' 'moving toward and reverting.' The Yellow Emperor's [victories] were a matter of human effort, that's all. Why was that?"
>
> Now, if there is a fortified city and one attacks it from the east and west but cannot take it and attacks from the south and north but cannot take it, can it be that all four directions failed to accord with an [auspicious] moment that could be exploited? If you still cannot take it, it's because the walls are high, the moats are deep, their weapons and implements fully prepared, their materials and grains accumulated in great quantities, and their valiant soldiers unified in their plans. If the wall is low, the moats shallow, and the defenses weak, then it can be taken. From this perspective, "moments," "seasons," and "Heavenly Offices" are not as important as human effort.

Just as Li Ch'üan's citation of Wang Mang's defeat and Chang Po-sung's stupidity, two *Wei Liao-tzu* chapters, "Martial Plans" and "Heavenly Offices," provide further explication by noting that King Wu's astonishing victory over Emperor Hsin of the Shang at the decisive battle of Mu-yeh had contravened basic wisdom about fortuitous and inimical deployments:

According to the *Heavenly Offices*, "deploying troops with water to the rear is referred to as 'isolated terrain.' Deploying troops facing a long ridge is termed 'abandoning the army.'" When King Wu attacked King Chou of the Shang, he deployed his troops with the Chi River behind him and confronted a mountain slope. With 22,500 men he attacked King Chou's hundreds of thousands and destroyed the Shang dynasty. Yet, hadn't King Chou deployed in accord with the Heavenly Offices?

Both sides had fought on the same day, making so-called auspicious and baleful days irrelevant. The surprising result is therefore discussed in terms that emphasize the uselessness of what would now be termed superstitious practices:

There was nothing auspicious nor abnormal, it was merely a case of perfecting oneself or not perfecting oneself in human affairs.

Generals of the present generation investigate "singular days" and "empty mornings," divine about Hsien-ch'ih, interpret full and disastrous days, accord with tortoise shell auguries, look for the auspicious and baleful, and observe the changes of the planets, constellations, and winds, wanting to thereby gain victory and establish their success. I view this as very difficult!

A second historical battle provided further confirmation of the need to confine one's energies to the human sphere:

The Ch'u general Kung-tzu Hsin was about to engage Ch'i in battle. At that time a comet appeared with its tail over Ch'i. [According to such beliefs,] wherever the tail pointed would be victorious and they could not be attacked.

Kung-tzu Hsin said: "What does a comet know? Those who fight according to the comet will certainly be overturned and conquered." On the morrow he engaged Ch'i and greatly defeated them. The Yellow Emperor said, "Putting spirits and ghosts first is not as good as first investigating my own knowledge." This means that the Heavenly Offices are nothing but human effort.

Accordingly, in "Combat Awesomeness" the *Wei Liao-tzu* asserted that "if you make the laws clear and are cautious in issuing orders, then without performing divination with the tortoise shell or milfoil you will obtain good fortune." Naturally, in a battlefield context, all omens, whether auspicious or baleful, were considered detrimental and measures had to be taken to proscribe prognostication as well as prevent the circulation of rumors about unusual phenomena such as birds flying backward.

The chapter also broaches the subject of *t'ien shih* (天 時), generally understood as the "seasons" (時) of Heaven but more comprehensively the appropriate moment or the time sanctioned for some activity. Extremely nebulous, the "Seasons of Heaven" might be interpreted as simply as contemporary weather conditions — heavy rain for example being inimical at the start of a campaign and clear and dry conditions correspondingly auspicious — or as complex as ongoing climatic manifestations including drought or extended periods of abnormal cold. However, in addition to some sort of abstract sanctioning, they were believed to vouchsafe an opportunity for significant action, especially by those who assumed that Heaven played an active role in human affairs. (This could be consciously, such as at the inception of a dynastic revolution prompted by the human plight, or mechanistically, in which case conditions just happened to be favorable.)

MINOR JOTTINGS:

Contrary to Li's normal practice, this chapter almost uniquely identifies the source of some of his material, obviating any need to ferret out the origins of his quotations and paraphrases.

Extensive discussion of the Shang's use of military divination may be found in my *Ancient Chinese Warfare*, and numerous cases of employing the *Yi Ching* for military purposes are preserved in the *Tso Chuan*, which remains available in James Legge's classic translation. The continuation of these practices in martial contexts despite Sun-tzu's rejection of nonhuman means and the evolution of other methods, especially those based on *ch'i* (vapor and cloud) manifestations, are discussed in my "Paradoxical Coexistence of Prognostication and Warfare." (Further examples of *ch'i* prognostication may be found in my "Martial Prognostication" in *Martial Culture in Imperial China*, while a broad consideration of early Chinese divination appears in Michael Loewe's seminal work, *Divination, Mythology and Monarchy in Han China*.)

The "straw dogs" passage appears in "Heaven and Earth Are Not Benevolent." Translations of the *Tao Te Ching* abound, but for a complete version interpreted in a specifically martial context see my *The Tao of War: The Martial Tao Te Ching*.

Numerous translations of Sun-tzu's *Art of War* have been made over the past century, including my own *Art of War* and General Griffith's similarly titled work. However, the only translation of the *Wei Liao-tzu* remains mine, included in the *Seven Military Classics of Ancient China*.

The legendary strategist Chiang T'ai Kung provided political and military advice to Kings Wen and Wu, the Chou dynasty's actual founders. However, although attributed to him, the *Liu-t'ao*, or *Six Secret Teachings*, is a vast compendium of material that probably reached final form toward the end of the Warring States period. (A complete translation may again be found in my *Seven Military Classics of Ancient China*.)

Wu Ch'i, with whom the *Wu-tzu* is normally identified, was an exemplary commander, administrator, and military thinker in the early Warring States period. (Translations of the *Wu-tzu* are included in my *Seven Military Classics of Ancient China* and General Griffith's *Art of War*.) According to the *Wu-tzu*, "While in command of the West River commandery, Wu Ch'i fought seventy-six major battles with the other feudal lords, winning sweeping victories in sixty-four of them and faring no worse than a draw in the remainder. He expanded Wei's land in all four directions, broadening its territory some thousand *li*." Thereafter he significantly reformed Ch'u's laws and successfully repelled threats from Ch'in.

Fan Li played a crucial role as a strategist and commander in King Kou-chien's revitalization of Yüeh after it had been vanquished by Wu. None of his writings survive, but the tale of Kou-chien's revenge clearly impressed Li Ch'üan because he cites it several times in the *T'ai-pai Yin-ching* and in his commentary to Sun-tzu's *Art of War*.

The *T'ai-pai Yin-ching*'s extensive ninety-third chapter is devoted to a discussion of the beliefs and measures employed in the highly complex *Tun-chia* (遁 甲) methodology despite the reliability of its indications being criticized here. Li's introduction to that material attempts to give it a somewhat realistic foundation in human affairs, but it really represents a very complex calendrical system with expansive implications for activities and deployments.

2

地 無 險 阻

"EARTH HAS NO RAVINES OR IMPEDIMENTS"

The classics state that "advantages of earth can be employed to assist the military." However, just like the movements of Heaven they cannot be relied upon.

Formerly the Three Miao had T'ung-t'ing Lake on the left and P'eng-li Lake on the right, but they did not cultivate virtue and righteousness, and Yü [of the Hsia] obliterated them. Thereafter, the place where [King] Chieh of the Hsia resided had the Yellow and Chi Rivers on the left, T'ai Hua [Hua-shan] on the right, the cliffs of Yi-ch'üeh in the south, and the slopes of Yang-ch'ang to the north. But in his practice of government, he did not cultivate benevolence, and King T'ang [of the Shang] displaced him. The state of [King] Chou of the Yin had Meng-men pass on the left, the T'ai-hang Mountains on the right, Mount Ch'ang to the north, and the great Yellow River flowing in the south, but he was dissipated, licentious, and neglected government affairs, and King Wu [of the Chou] killed him.

The land of Ch'in had Mount Yao and the Han-kuan pass on the left, Mounts Ch'ien and Lung on the right, Chung-nan and T'ai Hua to the fore, and Chiu-yüan and Shang-chün to the rear, but they were harsh and cruel in practicing punitive government, and Tzu Ying surrendered at Chih-tao. Subsequently [the Later Ch'in] ruler Yao Hung was captured at Pa-shang. The state of Wu occupied territory with five peaks to their south and three rivers to their north. They dwelled to the left of the sea's green waves and to the right of Mount Heng, but they did not reform their repressive government and the king of Wu lost his life in the end. Subsequently the ruler of Ch'en died at Ch'ang-ch'eng. The borders to Shu had Wu-hsia on the left and Ch'iung-po to the right, the impediment of the Lu River to the south, and the constricted passage of Chien-ko to the north, but at the time they did not have any heroes, so Liu Ch'an was unable to preserve [the state], and Li Shih was unable to solidify it.

From this perspective the movements of Heaven cannot provide good fortune to a ruler without the Tao, advantages of terrain cannot rescue a chaotic and doomed state. Whether the terrain is difficult or easy depends upon men. No terrain is [inherently] difficult or not difficult, easy or not easy. Survival and extinction lie in Virtue, warfare and defense lie in [exploiting the] terrain. Only worthy rulers and sagacious generals can preserve them these. What difficulty or easiness does the terrain [intrinsically] have?

SAWYER

This chapter forms a pair with the previous and the twelfth, "Esteeming Harmony," in exploring fundamental beliefs that pertain to the three realms of Heaven, Earth, and Man (as traditionally ordered). The terms *hsien* (險 "dangerous" or "difficult" in this context) and *tsu* (阻 "obstructive" or "impeded" in the title "*Ti Wu Hsien Tsu*") are just two of the types of terrain recognized in traditional Chinese martial theory. In "Initial Estimations," the *Art of War* states that "Earth encompasses far or near, difficult or easy, expansive or confined, fatal or tenable terrain." In discussing warfare's "four vital points" – *ch'i*, terrain, affairs, and strength – in the "The Tao of the General," Wu Ch'i noted that "when the road is narrow and the way perilous, famous mountains present great obstacles, and if ten men defend a place a thousand cannot pass, this is termed a 'vital point of earth.'"

Even though perspicacious commanders had long been implementing terrain-based tactics and it was well recognized that exploiting certain features could augment the least powerful force, the *Art of War* provides the earliest systematic correlation of operational principles and topographical characteristics. Nine terrains are generally associated with Sun-tzu because nine are described in a chapter of that name, but the *Art of War* actually describes some twenty distinct configurations while warning against several other deadly land formations that commanders ignored at their peril. Slighting the effects of simple grades, sand, wet ground, and other factors capable of exhausting an army could also prove costly.

Well cognizant of the impact of topographical features, the classic military writers all stressed the importance of exploiting the terrain's strategic characteristics. Thus it is not surprising that Li Ch'üan similarly focused on them in his "Configurations of Terrain" and mentions them in scattered chapters. Accordingly, his denial of any absolute impact is somewhat startling, if only because successfully traversing difficult terrain or breaking through naturally defined, well-defended obstacles would be costly if not tortuous. However, in concord with the overall thrust of the chapter, his intent was to dissuade people from believing that while topographical characteristics can facilitate or complicate military activities, their impact is neither unchangeable nor absolute. Moreover, he asserts that even though "warfare and defense lie in terrain," "survival and extinction lie in Virtue." Thus, in his conception features of terrain can enhance defensive efforts and leverage attacks, especially those undertaken by outnumbered forces, but they can still be negated without the wisdom, cohesiveness, and power brought about by virtuous and efficient rule.

In justification he cites several powerful states and dynasties that perished after having held sway over the realm for varying lengths of time, even hundreds of years, despite still possessing surpassing might. The Hsia and Shang, the first historically attested dynasties, both dwelled in comparatively secure topographical bastions, yet they quickly succumbed after the Virtue that had empowered the founders severely deteriorated and came to be displaced by hedonism, licentiousness, rampant perversity, and brutality. This caused enmity throughout the realm and brought about the disaffection of their own people, making it possible for the Shang to conquer the Hsia and the Chou to vanquish the Shang, both in decisive single battles despite having been seriously outnumbered. Even more dramatically the short-lived Ch'in, which had just unified the empire after centuries of struggle and thereby ended the Warring States period, quickly perished when the entire populace rebelled. Just as the Chou, Ch'in's rise had been facilitated by their location within the protective confines of the Wei River valley, where their remoteness and the largely impervious mountain ranges deterred even the most aggressive forces.

Minor Jottings:

The first paragraph denying that the terrain could convey insurmountable strategic advantages was adopted from a famous persuasion purportedly offered by Wu Ch'i that is now preserved in his *Shih Chi* biography. However, Li expanded it with additional examples from the Ch'in and the Later Ch'in dynasties to make it more relevant for T'ang readers.

3

人 無 湧 怯

"MEN HAVE NEITHER COURAGE NOR FEAR"

The classics state that courage and fear are a matter of human nature, strength and weakness a matter of terrain. Men from Ch'in are said to be fierce, those from Chin resolute, from Wu fearful, from Shu timid, from Ch'u insubstantial, from Ch'i very deceitful, from Yüeh flighty, from the Hai-tai region robust, from around the K'ung-t'ung mountains martial, from Yen and Chao fervent, from the Ch'ien and Lung mountain area courageous, and from Han and Wei generous. Accordingly, [it is believed that] what the configuration of the terrain gives birth to and human *ch'i* absorbs are courage and fear.

Actually, courage and fear lie in planning, strength, and weakness in the strategic configuration of power. When plans are effective and strategic power replete, the fearful become courageous; when plans are snatched away and strategic power lost, the courageous become fearful.

17

With regard to assertions that the men of Ch'in are fierce, the prince of Shen-t'u was defeated at Yao-kuan and Tu Hung's general routed at the Hsi River, so how can the men of Ch'in be termed fierce?

As for the men of Wu being fearful, the armies of Fu-ch'ai, king of Wu, were unmatched throughout the realm. They defeated Ch'i at Ai-ling, and Wu became leader [of the states] in Chin's stead at the conclave of Huang-ch'ih (Yellow Lake), so how can the men of Wu be said to have been fearful?

As for the men of Shu being timid, Chu-ko K'ung-ming (Chu-ko Liang) gathered the masses of Pa and Shu and led the army in strikes into the central plains. Even as a corpse, his awesomeness affected Wei's generals, so how can the men of Shu be termed wavering?

As for the men of Ch'u being insubstantial, Hsiang Yü destroyed Ch'in, made a prisoner of Wang Li, and slew Su Chiao. His majesty overspread all the territory within the four seas, the feudal lords crouched down in submission, none even daring to glance upward, so how can the men of Ch'u be called insubstantial?

As for the men of Ch'i being deceitful, T'ien Heng motivated five hundred death-defying warriors to race eastward to an island in the sea. When Heng committed suicide [rather than submit to the Han], they all fell on their swords the same day, so how can the men of Ch'i be said to be deceitful?

As for the men of Yüeh being flighty, with [nothing more than the] remnants of a lost state, Kou-chien, king of Yüeh, nurtured his masses of old and weak [survivors] and in nine years extinguished Wu. In attacking the strong with the weak, seizing the large with the small, can Yüeh really be termed flighty?

As for the men of Yen and Chao being fervent, Ch'ih Yu was defeated at Chuo-li, Yen Tan died at the Yi River, Wang Chün was [captured and] tied up at the gate of Su, and the Kung-sun were exterminated at Shang-ku, so how can Yen and Chao be termed fervent?

Therefore what is termed courage and fear lies in laws, success and defeat repose in wisdom. When you employ punishments, the fearful become courageous, and when you employ rewards, the courageous die [fighting]. What can shift men's fear and change their hearts (minds) is found in punishments and rewards. In what sense are courage and fear intrinsically found in men?

SAWYER

The concept of regionalism noted at the chapter's outset probably predates the Shang dynasty, having evolved when travel beyond the nuclear area of Chinese culture revealed startling differences in topography and vegetation. According to the *Ssu-ma Fa*, "Men from each [of the four] quarters have their own nature. Character differs from region to region. Through teaching they come to have regional habits, the customs of each state [thus] being different. [Only] through the Tao are their customs transformed."

However, the earliest expression of regional theory has traditionally been attributed to the *Shang Shu*, which depicts Yü the Great, one of China's mythical cultural heroes and the Hsia dynasty's legendary progenitor, dividing China into nine regions that were characterized in terms of soil type, field productivity, and inhabitants.

The inception of yin and yang and the five phases — two fundamental concepts of Chinese protoscience that could also be employed to classify phenomenal occurrences and interpret their patterns — quickly resulted in correlating cycles of seasonal activity, earthly directions, and important regional differences including habits and personality under them in the Warring States period. Insofar as the different states were expected to manifest diverse temperaments, tastes, and behavioral tendencies (such as being easily angered) rather than remaining merely descriptive, regionalism acquired political and projective implications. (This thinking is clearly reflected in the characterizations of fighting tendencies preserved in the *Hsün-tzu*, *Wu-tzu*, and other texts.) The concept eventually became so pervasive that the correlated characterizations even influenced traditional military science and strategic planning.

The crux of the chapter lies in the two paragraphs that open and close the discussion. In the former Li asserts that "courage and fear lie in planning, strength, and weakness in the strategic configuration of power" and in the latter that "what is termed courage and fear lie in laws, success and defeat repose in wisdom." However, although Li differed on the nature of fear and courage, throughout the *T'ai-pai Yin-ching* he never fully rejects the regional characterizations, including when comparing the righteousness and martial capabilities of the various states in the chapter titled "Excelling in Command." Nevertheless, he apparently felt compelled to refute the idea that courage and fear are indelibly predetermined and argue instead for emotional malleability under the compulsive influence of governmental measures. Thus much of the chapter is devoted to undermining particular assertions, such as that Wu's warriors were fearful. However, the events he cites are singular and often occurred at the end of a state's tale and thus do not negate the characterization's general validity.

The complex concept of strategic power (*shih* 勢) that figures prominently in ancient military and Legalist thought perhaps originated in the former and is one of the *Art of War*'s defining concepts. A wide variety of terms have been used to translate *shih* and approximate the concept's various meanings, including "circumstances," "latent energy," "shape," "strength," "momentum," "tactical power," "force," and "power." However, in essence it combines the concepts of power and positional advantage and might be best understood in our translation as the "strategic configuration of power."

The *Art of War*'s analogy of a log or stone perched atop a hill is particularly appropriate because its potential energy can be explosively released:

> One who employs strategic power commands men in battle as if he were rolling logs and stones. The nature of wood and stone is to be quiet when stable but to move when on precipitous ground. If they are square they stop, if round they tend to move. Thus the strategic power of one who excels at

employing men in warfare is comparable to rolling round boulders down a thousand-fathom mountain. Such is the strategic configuration of power.

Accordingly, commanders would seek to maneuver the army into a position where the impact of its "strategically configured power" would be like the sudden onrush of water cascading down from a mountain peak, or, as imagized in "Strategic Military Power," "The strategic configuration of power [is visible in] the onrush of pent-up water tumbling stones along."

The statement that "one who employs strategic power commands men in battle as if he were rolling logs and stones" underlies Li's assertion in this chapter and in his commentary to the *Art of War* that strategic power encompasses the men and radically affects their emotional state: "When plans are effective and strategic power replete, the fearful become courageous; when plans are snatched away and strategic power lost, the courageous become fearful." However, in his view strategic power alone cannot forge this result but acts in conjunction with effective plans that presumably inspire confidence. (It should be noted that Li was probably less sanguine about the possibility of fear being changed to courage because in his commentary to the *Art of War*'s "Strategic Military Power" he advises assigning men to various roles based upon their courage or lack of it, the naturally timid being deployed in defensive work.)

Despite these assertions, Li also championed the necessity of punishments and rewards because "when you employ punishments, the fearful become courageous, and when you employ rewards, the courageous will die." (Unspoken is what constitutes "courage" and "fear" or whether the emotional aspect is even relevant as long as men perform effectively in combat situations.) By the T'ang dynasty, China had already long pondered the nature of courage and developed systematic psychological measures for eliciting it such as the feasts that will be described in "Inciting the Warriors," as well as for deterring the fearful from failing to act. As framed by Shang Yang, Han Fei-tzu, and in the *Wei Liao-tzu*, rewards were considered necessary to stimulate daring behavior, strong punishments being the sole means to prevent cowardice and flight.

Accordingly, in a typical formulation found in "Orders for Severe Punishments," the *Wei Liao-tzu* confidently asserts that "if you cause the people to fear heavy punishments within the state, then outside the state they will regard the enemy lightly. Thus the Former Kings made the regulations and measures clear before making their awesomeness and punishments heavy. When punishments are heavy, they will fear them within the state. When they fear them within the state, they will be stalwart outside it." Or, as stated in "Tactical Balance of Power in Attacks," "The people do not have two things that they fear equally. If they fear us, they will despise the enemy. If they fear the enemy, they will despise us. The one who is despised will be defeated, the one who established his awesomeness will be victorious."

Achieving the requisite battlefield performance was further ensured by imposing a mutual guarantee system that extended across the squads of five and vertically implicated the officers in an ever-expanding hierarchy. Death was frequently inflicted for even relatively minor infractions but invariably for defeat, flight, or the loss of a comrade within the web of responsibility. (Although recognizing the need for deterrence, the *Six Secret Teachings* and the other classic martial texts apart from the *Wei Liao-tzu* tend to emphasize motivational factors such as benevolence, righteousness, and Virtuous government over punishments.)

MINOR JOTTINGS

In his commentary to the *Art of War*, Li Ch'üan notes that the drums control the courageous and fearful.

Traditional Chinese views on courage, which were never singular, are discussed in my "Martial Qi in China: Courage and Spirit in Thought and Military Practice," *Journal of Military and Strategic Studies*, Winter 2008/2009, available at www.jmss.org.

Examples of the sort of draconian regulations and severe punishments that prevailed in the Warring States period and probably earlier are preserved in the last twelve chapters of the *Wei Liao-tzu*.

Li Ch'üan was particularly interested in the epic clashes between Fu-ch'ai of Wu and Kou-chien of Yüeh and Hsiang Yü and Liu Pang. They reappear in subsequent chapters and in the examples he employs for his commentary to the *Art of War*.

Although he nominally directed five northward invasions during the early Three Kingdoms period intended to prevent Shu's extinction by unopposed invaders, Chu-ko Liang (Zhuge Liang) is best known as a consummate strategist and tactical innovator.

Finally, several clauses have obviously dropped out of the text because Li fails to contravene the conventional assessment of the men from Han, Wei, and the Liang and Lung area.

4

主 有 道 德

"THE RULER POSSESSES THE TAO AND TE"

The [*Huai-nan Tzu*] states that when the Three August Ones gained full [comprehension] of the Tao and established [themselves] in centrality, their spirits transformed and roamed about in order to give comfort to the four quarters, but no one in the realm attributed the accomplishment to them. The Five Emperors took their principles from Heaven and modeled on Earth. They spoke and issued commands, and All under Heaven enjoyed great tranquility, but rulers and ministers yielded credit for the achievement to each other.

When the Tao and Virtue were abandoned, kings appeared who valued benevolence and righteousness. When benevolence and righteousness were abandoned, hegemons appeared who esteemed knowledge and strength. When knowledge and strength were abandoned, the Warring States resulted and deception and deceit arose.

When the Tao of sagacious men proved inadequate for governing, they employed laws; when laws proved insufficient for governing, they employed techniques; when techniques proved inadequate to govern, they employed authority; when authority proved inadequate to govern, they used power. Once power was employed, the large annexed the small.

In antiquity the Chou established eighteen hundred feudal lords, but they were eventually reduced to six states. When the six states employed their chariots and troops to resolve difficulties, warfare arose. It wasn't that the rulers of the six states [wanted to] reject Tao and *Te* (Virtue) and embrace authority and power, but when authority and power come into use, they must be embraced. When the Tao and *Te* have been abandoned, they must be rejected. It is inescapably so.

Only sages can go back to the beginning and return to the foundation, can administer the state with uprightness (*cheng* 正) and employ the military with the unorthodox (*ch'i* 奇) and thereby govern All under Heaven without perturbations. Uprightness [consists of] names and laws, the unorthodox [consists of] authority (*ch'üan* 權) and techniques (*shu* 術). If the state is governed with names and laws, the myriad things cannot become chaotic. If the army is employed with authority and techniques, none in the realm will prove successful as enemies. If one governs the realm without affairs, the myriad things will not be able to cause agitation. If they do not cause agitation, spirit will be clear. Clarity of spirit is the source of wisdom, placidity of wisdom the repository of mind. When the spirit is clear and wisdom placid, the myriad things can be given form. When the ruler of men knows the nature of the myriad things, he can shoulder and employ them, and then neither perfected nor menial men will lose their positions.

When Virtue is ample but position inferior, it is termed excessive, when Virtue is minimal but position honored, it is termed loss. It is better to be excessive in the person of the perfected man rather than suffer loss with the menial man. When it is excessive in the perfected man, men are deficient in principle, but when it is lost in the menial man, the myriad things incur misfortune.

Thus it is said that people do not use flowing water as a mirror but instead still water because of its clarity and tranquility. When the ruler's Tao is clear and tranquil, he will not lose any talent in assigning responsibilities, and the six bureaus will all preserve their responsibilities.

Within the four borders, the affairs of the hundred surnames are entrusted to the prime minister; outside the borders the affairs of enemy states are entrusted to the (commanding) general. A saying holds that when ministers and generals are perspicacious, the state will not [employ] the army. Emperor Shun subjugated the Yu Miao with [a dance] of shields and axes, and the state of Lu attracted the Huai Yi with a university. Those who achieve victory through the Tao are emperors, those who gain victory through Virtue are kings, those who achieve it through strategy are hegemons, and those who achieve victory through force are strong. The armies of the strong [will inevitably be] exterminated and the armies of hegemons severed, but the armies of emperors and kings will have no enemies before them. Believe that the Tao of rulers is thus!

SAWYER

This chapter reflects Li's vacillation between wanting to believe, and therefore asserting, that Virtue can be sufficient yet grudgingly recognizing that even Virtue had become inadequate in the face of power and violence because the times had changed. Despite the carnage all about him, Mencius had long ago asserted that the benevolent have no enemies before them. His view, however naïve, continued to be cited in imperial court discussions whenever bureaucratic factions sought to oppose regal inclinations to external military action, particularly after Chu Hsi's impetus essentially sanctified Mencius's teachings in the Sung. However, it failed to hold sway in the T'ang, which had been founded after centuries of violence and witnessed the specter of An Lu-shan's highly destructive rebellion.

Li actually begins by adopting a few lines from the opening paragraph of "Yüan Tao," the initial (and in many ways, defining) chapter of the *Huai-nan Tzu*, the eclectic text that embraces but is not limited to the philosophy and concepts embodied in the somewhat earlier *Tao Te Ching*. With its discussion of actionless action, speculation on form and spirit, and ethereal disquisitions on a decidedly naturalistic, often transcendent approach to life and government, the *Huai-nan Tzu* clearly had great appeal for Li Ch'üan, and he seems to have been thoroughly familiar with its complex teachings. However, even though he incorporates selected statements and adapts some of the phrasing to other purposes, the T'ang's undeniably violent heritage prevented him from fully embracing its teachings.

Somewhat surprisingly, the *Huai-nan Tzu* contains a lengthy section on military affairs that not only depicts warfare as necessary but inherent to humankind. Moreover, it was in response to inimical human tendencies that the Sages felt compelled to arise and impose controls, however selflessly undertaken:

> When the ancients employed the military, it was not to profit from broadening their lands or because they coveted gold and jade. It was to preserve those (about to) perish, continue the severed, pacify the chaos under Heaven, and eliminate the harm affecting the myriad people.
>
> Now, as for the beasts that have blood and *ch'i*, teeth and horns, claws in front and spurs in back: those with horns butt, those with teeth bite, those with poison sting, and those with hooves kick. When happy they play with each other, when angry they harm each other. This is their Heavenly nature.
>
> Men have a desire for food and clothes, but things are insufficient to supply them. Thus they group together in diverse places. When the division (of things) is not equitable, they fervently seek them and conflict arises. When there is conflict the strong coerce the weak and the courageous encroach upon the fearful. Since men do not have the

strength of sinews and bone or the sharpness of claws and teeth, they cut leather to make armor and smelt iron to make blades. (In antiquity) men who were greedy, obtuse, and avaricious destroyed and pillaged all under Heaven. The myriad people were disturbed and moved, none could be at peace in his place. Sages suddenly arose to punish the strong and brutal and pacify a chaotic age. They eliminated danger and got rid of the corrupt, turning the muddy into the clear, danger into peace.

Other writings from the Warring States and Former Han (such as the eclectic *Lü-shih Ch'un-ch'iu*) similarly asserted that despite being paragons of Virtue, the early Sages were compelled to enact powerful measures. Although probably never able to access the *Military Methods*, Li Ch'üan would certainly have affirmed Sun Pin's views:

At the time when Yao possessed All under Heaven, there were seven (tribes) who dishonored the king's edicts and did not put them into effect. [It was not possible for Yao] to be at ease and attain the profit [of governing All under Heaven]. He was victorious in battle, and his strength was established; therefore, All under Heaven submitted.

In antiquity Shen Nung did battle with the Fu and Sui; the Yellow Emperor did battle [with Ch'ih Yu] at Shu-lü; Yao attacked Kung Kung; Shun attacked Ch'e; and [Yü] drove off the Three Miao. T'ang deposed Chieh; King Wu attacked Chou [Emperor Hsin of the Shang]; and the Duke of Chou obliterated (the remnant state of) Shang-yen when it rebelled. Thus if someone's virtue is not like that of the Five Emperors, his ability does not reach that of the Three Kings, nor his wisdom match that of the Duke of Chou [yet he] says, "I want to accumulate benevolence and righteousness, practice the rites and music, and wear flowing robes and thereby prevent conflict and seizure," it is not that Yao and Shun did not want this, but they could not attain it. Therefore they mobilized the military to constrain (the evil).

For example, in his "Planning for the State," Wu Ch'i similarly asserted that the legendary Sage rulers had imposed their Virtue through force rather than numinosity:

> In antiquity the ruler of the Ch'eng Sang clan cultivated Virtue but neglected military affairs, thereby leading to the extinction of his state. The ruler of the Yu Hu clan relied upon his masses and loved courage and thus lost his ancestral altars. The enlightened ruler, observing this, will certainly nourish culture and Virtue within the domestic sphere while putting his military preparations in order in response to external situations. Thus, when opposing an enemy force, if you do not advance, you haven't attained righteousness. When the dead lie stiff and you grieve for them, you haven't attained benevolence.

As mentioned in the introduction, Wang Chen turned to the *Tao Te Ching* for lessons in how conflict might be ended, but in this context Li felt compelled to acknowledge the need for both strong governments and vigorous military forces. However, both of them accepted the *Tao Te Ching*'s depiction of ongoing devolution. According to "The Great Tao Abandoned":

> The Great Tao being abandoned,
> There is benevolence and righteousness.
> Knowledge and wisdom coming forth,
> There is great artifice.
> The six human relations being disharmonious,
> There is filiality and parental love.
> The state being confused and turbulent,
> There are loyal ministers.

Another well-known chapter, "Superior Virtue Is Not Virtuous," emphasizes the actionless nature of Superior Virtue while decrying the conflict that ultimately results from its loss:

Superior Virtue is not virtuous so is Virtuous.
Inferior Virtue does not lose virtue so is without Virtue.
Superior Virtue is actionless, without external objective,
Inferior Virtue is actionless but has external objectives.
Superior benevolence is implemented but without any objective,
Superior righteousness is practiced with an objective.
Superior rites are implemented but if there is no response,
Arms are bared to coerce one.
Thus only after the Tao has been lost is there Virtue,
Only after Virtue has been lost is there benevolence,
Only after benevolence has been lost is there righteousness,
Only after righteousness has been lost is there ritual.
Now ritual is the veneer of loyalty and sincerity, the start
of chaos.

Consonant with this view and the introductory passages of this chapter, the eclectic *Three Strategies* outlined a highly similar version in introducing its "Middle Strategy":

Now, the Three August Ones never spoke, but their transformations flowed throughout the Four Seas. Thus the world had no one to whom to attribute the accomplishments.

The Emperors embodied Heaven and took Earth as their model. They spoke and issued orders, and the world attained Great Peace. Ruler and minister yielded the credit for this to each other while all within the Four Seas were transformed without the common people being conscious of how the changes came about. Therefore in employing subordinates they did not rely on the forms of propriety or rewards. There was the beauty of accomplishments and no harm.

Kings governed men by means of the Tao, causing their hearts to be compliant and their wills to be submissive, while also establishing restrictive measures and making preparations against decline. All the feudal lords within the Four Seas assembled at their courts, and the duty of kingship was not neglected. Even though they made military preparations,

31

they never suffered the misfortune of warfare. Rulers did not doubt their subordinates, subordinates had faith in their rulers. The state was settled, the ruler secure, and bureaucrats could resign with righteousness, so they also were able to have beauty without harm.

The hegemons governed their officers by virtue of authority, bonding them through trust, motivating them with rewards. When that trust declined, the officers grew distant, and when rewards became inadequate, they would not submit to orders.

In chapter nine, "Esteeming Harmony," Li comes closest to embracing Mencius's idea that Virtue is sufficient, even though he recognizes variant approaches and differences in effectiveness: "Rulers who have penetrated the Tao are able to subjugate others through Virtue. Benevolent rulers are able to harmonize people with righteousness; wise rulers are able to gain victory over others through strength; rulers who rely upon authority are able to control men through power." Although he still entertained visions of actionless sagely administration (just as the *Tao Te Ching* describes), Li well recognized that "authority and power" had come to the fore, and their effects could not be forestalled.

(Some commentators have historically understood the last lines of "The Ruler Possesses the Tao and *Te*" as reading, "The armies of the strong will exterminate those of the hegemons and sever the armies of emperors and have no enemies before them." Although not impossible, it would be at variance with the conquest hierarchy that Li puts forward in "Excelling in Command" as well as grammatically different from the form that "those who do something are X.")

5

國 有 富 強

"THE WEALTHY AND STRONG STATE"

The [*Shang-chün Shu*] asserts that "states become rich and strong through vigorously investigating the nature of authority in order to firmly grasp the handles [of power] and thoroughly examining the nature of methods in order to control men." Stimulating agriculture is a matter of techniques; wealth lies in grain. Planning for warfare is a matter of authority; strength lies in the army.

Thus [the *Shang-chün Shu*] states that "when mobilizing the army to attack the rebellious, responsibility is entrusted to martial ranks. When martial ranks [are well ordered], the army will be strong. When the army is drawn down, agriculture and sericulture can be encouraged; when agriculture and sericulture are encouraged, the state will be rich." States that do not take the measure of their terrain will fail to become rich, armies that do not employ plans will not succeed in achieving strength.

In antiquity sagacious men modeled on Heaven and became kings, worthy rulers modeled on Earth and became emperors, and knowledgeable rulers took men as their measure and became hegemons. States become rich and strong by taking advantage of the seasons, relying upon the resources of earth, and employing the strength of men. "Taking advantage of the seasons of Heaven" means planting grain in the spring and [letting it] mature in the summer, planting wheat in the autumn and harvesting and storing it away in the winter. As for the profits derived from Earth, if a state has abundant, fertile lands but the people do not have enough to eat, it means that the requisite farming implements were not properly prepared; if a state derives profits from the mountains and seas but the people lack wealth, it is because commercial travelers are insufficient.

Those who circulate precious and distinctive things from the four quarters so that places that have them can exchange them in places that lack them are termed commercial travelers. Those who exert their strength so as to maximize the land's wealth and then employ it to sustain the army are termed farmers. Those who put silk and hemp [threads] in order to make clothes are referred to as female workers.

Fur and feathers from Yün-meng; cinnabar pebbles from Ch'ien-ch'i; leather and horns from Ching-yang; cedar and catalpa from Chiang-heng; bamboo arrows from K'uai-chi; fish, salt, rugs, and felt robes from Yen and Ch'i; lacquer and hemp from Ch'ung and Yü; knives from Cheng; axes from Sung; adzes from Lu; swords from Wu; horn from Yen; small bamboos from Ching; arrow shafts from the Fen and Ho River regions; and the copper and tin from Wu and Yüeh are the wealth of Earth. Chuo in Yen, Han-tan in Chao, Wen in Wei, Ying-yang in Han, Lin-tzu in Ch'i, Wan-ch'iu in Ch'en, Yang-ti in Cheng, the two Chou in Luo, Chü-ch'u in Yüeh, Yün-meng in Ch'u, Chü-lu in Ch'i, and Meng-chü in Sung are all superlative places.

Dwelling in similar circumstances, unless the impoverished suffered the misfortune of natural disasters or infectious diseases, they must have either been lazy or extravagant. There are no unusual occupations in this world that lead to being singularly wealthy. If a state is wealthy, it is because the people have been parsimonious or exerted themselves.

Differences in poverty and wealth among states that were originally comparable result in them becoming rulers and subjects. Differences in strength and weakness result in states of the same noble patrimony annexing each other. Differences in strength and weakness among states with comparable terrain result from chaos and order. If they are governed by the Tao and have sufficient land to encompass the populace, great affairs can be achieved. If they have markets and products circulate, goods and wealth can be accumulated.

When there is adequate dwelling space, the wise will never speak about weakness; where the markets produce profits, the wise will not speak about poverty. If the land is thoroughly exploited, you will never worry about lacking wealth; if the people are strictly employed, you need not fear [being unable to mount] a strong defense. Thus the [Sage Emperor] Shen Nung taught people to plow and became king of the realm; T'ang [of the Shang] and Wu [of the Chou] engaged in warfare and subjugated the feudal lords.

If the state suffers from stupidity, wisdom can strengthen it; if the state is wise, force can strengthen the people. By employing wisdom you can be strong within and rich without; by employing force you can be rich within and strong without. Thus Emperor Wu-ti of the Han pacified the Nan Yüeh and turned the area into an imperial garden. He drove off the Ch'iang and Hu, turning the territory into a hunting park. Precious treasures and exquisite curios filled the inner palace, famous horses with names such as T'ao T'u and K'uai T'i crowded the stables. Ordinary people rode in well-built carriages with excellent horses and were surfeited with grapefruit and oranges. This is what is termed wisdom bringing about strength within and wealth without.

Duke Hsiao of Ch'in issued commands to reclaim fallow land and prohibited merchants from being able to buy grain and farmers from selling it. He eliminated the hostels for foreigners and closed the marshes and mountains. He made the price of wine and meat expensive and doubled the imposts at the passes and in the markets, resulting in farmers being at ease and merchants laboring. After [these policies] had been implemented for several years, the granaries and storehouses were full, and people knew the proper forms of behavior (*li*) and righteousness. When Ch'in Shih-huang employed them as his resources and proceeded eastward, he was able to swallow up all the feudal lords. This is what is referred to as force producing riches within and strength without.

One who understands the nature of hegemony and kingship knows that without wisdom a state cannot engage in warfare, without agriculture the state cannot be sustained. It has never been the case that [a state] attained riches and strength through other means.

SAWYER

Although *fu-kuo ch'iang-ping* (富 國 強 兵), "enrich the state and strengthen the army," has been a much-ballyhooed Chinese watchword in recent centuries, in both the formative Warring States period and Li Ch'üan's era the idea that the state's wealth should be increased through commercial activities was rarely raised. The well-known Confucian disparagement of the merchant class, which held sway from the Han onward, may never have prevented people from pursuing riches, but it could cause their ostracization and often prompted official attempts to constrain conspicuous displays of wealth. In the Warring States period, it was Shang Yang's antimercantile thinking that heavily influenced the state of Ch'in. Almost paradoxically, Li begins by paraphrasing selected statements from the *Shang-chün Shu*, the book that purportedly preserves Shang Yang's teachings, before surprisingly going on to emphasize that the foundation of all wealth is a vibrant economy marked by energetic trading activities: "If they have markets and products circulate, good and wealth can be accumulated."

Despite not being particularly effusive, the classic military writings were not totally bereft of this idea. In particular, in "Martial Plans" the *Wei Liao-tzu* notes:

36

If [the state's resources] are neither sufficient to go forth to wage battle nor adequate to remain within the borders and defend the state, [the insufficiency] must be corrected with markets. Markets are the means to provide for both offensive and defensive warfare. If a state of ten thousand chariots lacks states of a thousand chariots to assist it, it must have markets able to furnish a hundred chariots.

Now, markets are offices for sundry goods. [The government should] buy items in the market that are cheap and sell those that have grown expensive in order to restrain the aristocrats and people. People eat one *tou* of grain while horses eat three *tou* of beans, so why do the people have a famished look and the horses appear emaciated? The markets have goods to deliver, but the office lacks a controller. Now, if you raise the best trained army under Heaven but don't manage the sundry goods, this is not what is referred to as being able to conduct warfare.

Although he was subsequently much reviled by orthodox historians and Confucian-influenced thinkers, Shang Yang's infamous revision of Ch'in's laws and administrative ordinances contributed substantially to central government efforts directed toward increasing the state's economic strength and military power. Vehemently opposed to concepts of virtue, righteousness, and compassion as well as to what he viewed as the deleterious effects of historical learning and disparate values, Shang Yang emphasized unity in belief, enriching the state solely through farming, and making all rank—and thus advancement—dependent upon agricultural achievement and battlefield performance.

Even as the merchants were being thwarted, immigrants were encouraged to come to Ch'in because it had a large territory but only a limited population. Shang Yang even envisioned distributing the populace in accord with the terrain's potential. Although some 40 percent would reside in cities and towns, the remainder would be appropriately dispersed throughout the mountains, forests, marshes, and open landscape. Moreover, in his conception the populace would be controlled by laws enforced with rewards and punishments, the two handles of administrative power, with the latter being emphasized.

The classic military writings all concur in stressing the people's welfare and stimulating agriculture so as to provide the material basis for both ordinary life and warfare. According to "Preserving the State's Territory" in the *Six Secret Teachings*, "the ruler must focus upon developing wealth within his state. Without material wealth he has nothing with which to be benevolent. If he does not bespread beneficence, he will have nothing with which to bring his relatives together. If he estranges his relatives, it will be harmful. If he loses the common people, he will be defeated." In "Combat Awesomeness" the *Wei Liao-tzu* similarly proclaims that "land is the means for nourishing the populace; [fortified] cities the means for defending the land; and combat the means for defending the cities. Thus if you concentrate upon plowing, the people will not be hungry; if you concentrate upon defense, the land will not be endangered; if you concentrate upon combat, the cities will not be encircled. These three were the fundamental concerns of the Former Kings, and among them military affairs were the most urgent."

A second chapter in the *Wei Liao-tzu*, "Discussion of Regulations," further describes the situation in the ideal state: "We should cause that apart from engaging in agriculture there will be no means to eat and apart from engaging in battle there will be no means to attain rank. We should cause the people to bump into each other in competing to go out to the farms and into battle. Then under Heaven we will not have any enemies!" A third chapter, "Military Discussions," summarizes the beneficial effects: "When the land is broad and under cultivation, the state will be wealthy; when the people are numerous and well-ordered, the state will be governed. When the state is wealthy and well governed, although the people do not remove the blocks [from their chariots] nor expose their armor, their awesomeness instills order on All under Heaven."

Li Ch'üan somewhat revisits the topic of wisdom and strength by unexpectedly extolling the famous Martial Emperor (Wu Ti) of the Former Han dynasty for having achieved profitable conquests even though his accomplishments are highly discordant with Li's inclination toward Virtue-based subjugation. Han Wu-ti embarked on a series of so-called punitive—but actually highly expansionist—campaigns into the steppe region and Central Asia in strengths up to two hundred thousand troops. Although they conquered vast territory and created the possibility of the earliest "silk route," they also bankrupted the state and depleted its military resources.

MINOR JOTTINGS:

The first paraphrase from the *Shang-chün Shu* is essentially derived from "Calculating the Terrain," a chapter that stresses the importance of agriculture, while the second is from "Eliminating Strength."

Some of the products described in the middle section are taken from a passage incorporated in the *Chou Li*, a work compiled in the Former Han that purportedly records the organization and ritual practices of the preceding Chou dynasty.

Within a purely military context, the term translated as "authority" (*ch'üan* 權) usually refers to a tactical imbalance of power. First formulated in the *Art of War*, it quickly became a core concept in early Chinese military science, and achieving a favorable imbalance remains a chief objective of contemporary PRC military science for fighting localized conflicts under high-tech conditions.

6

賢　有　遇　時

"THE WORTHY ENCOUNTER THE TIMES"

The classics state that when worthy men are born into the world, they do not necessarily have any particular nationality or esteemed clan ancestry, nor do they have an unusual appearance or manifest exceptional knowledge or courage. Some appear wise, some stupid; some dazed, some perceptive. You cannot seek them in the traces of affairs, you cannot discern them by reputation or accomplishments. Only the mind of an enlightened ruler can discover them through their Tao being the same, their intentions united, their good faith matching, and words being fully in accord. It is similar to pouring water onto the ground insofar as it first flows toward dampness or setting a fire out in the plains, which first [ignites] the dry materials.

For example, Yi Yin was a farmer among the Hsin and a wine steward during Chieh's rule of the Hsia, but King T'ang found him serving among his cooks and acquired his services, allowing him to rise up and displace Chieh. The T'ai Kung was a butcher at Chao-ko and sold soy sauce at Chi-chin, but when the Chou acquired his services after dangling a fishing line, they killed Emperor Hsin [King Chou of the Shang] and subsequently captured [his rebellious successor] Wu Keng.

With his hair disheveled and feet bare, Wu Yün (Wu Tzu-hsü) clasped his bow and arrows under his arm and went to Wu to beg for food. Having heard of his fame and admired his righteousness, King Ho-lü descended from the dais to receive him, spoke with him for three days, and never had another doubt.

Fan Li was born in a wasteland with five houses. When he was young, his inner senses seemed blind and he reacted to sounds as if deaf. At the time the people all regarded him as extremely mad, but when Ta-fu Chung came and saw him, he knew he was a worthy and therefore knocked on the door to invite him to return with him to the "gate of earth" (Nan Yüeh).

Kuan Yi-wu (Kuan Chung) was brought back to Ch'i from Lu in bonds, but Duke Huan of Ch'i entrusted him with premiership; Pai Li-hsi sold gruel in Chin, but Duke Mu of Ch'in entrusted him with the government; and Han Hsin was a deserter from Nan-cheng and [known as] the fearful fellow of Huai-yang, but Emperor Han Kao-tsu had him return with him to plan strategy.

Thus it is said that if the ruler's mind is like a bright mirror or a clear pool of spring water, round and enlightened within while giving shape to things on the exterior, he can employ the worthy and entrust the capable with responsibility without losing the moment. But if he lacks mental perceptivity and clarity of wisdom and instead relies on the vision of other men and listens with their ears, he will be like an old fellow with murky sight trying to discern colorful embroidered clothes or someone with distorted or no hearing trying to listen to Shao-hua's melody. Neither dark black nor yellow nor [the notes] *kung* and *wei* penetrate their minds. It has never been possible for anyone to be like this yet want to acquire [talented] men and become hegemon.

Thus the Five Emperors penetrated the Tao and flourished, King Chieh [of the Hsia] and King Chou [of the Shang] neglected the Tao and were abandoned. The Tao of abandonment and flourishing lies in the mind of the ruler and in gaining the employment of worthies, not in military forces that are strong, land that is expansive, people that are numerous, or states that are rich.

SAWYER

Although never bereft of obligatory assertions about the importance of the ruler's Virtue in establishing beneficent government, the classic military writings and many Warring States political works including the *Hsün-tzu* and *Mo-tzu* emphasized the importance of identifying and attracting worthy (and of course talented) men. Wu-tzu, for example, felt that "if you are able to have worthy men hold high positions and the unworthy occupy low positions, then your battle formations will already be stable." As already noted, as warfare increased in scope and lethality in the latter part of the Spring and Autumn just before exploding in the Warring States period, survival became dependent upon acquiring and effectively employing men with outstanding intellectual capabilities for both civil tasks and increasingly professionalized military command roles.

However, it is not just "worthy" men—men of skill, mental acuity, and other talents—that are the focus of this chapter but "Worthies." Nearly synonymous with Sages, they are primarily distinguished by their surpassing moral nature. (Both were necessarily men of Virtue, but Sages were thought to have surpassing wisdom and nearly transcendental power, even though their perceptivity in later ages no longer matched that of the ancient paragons.) Worthies were traditionally identified with Confucianism, but a careful examination of the extant text attributed to Confucius, the *Lun Yü*, particularly the more authentic portions, reveals that he said remarkably little about their nature. Even Mencius offered only a couple of observations, including (in VIIB12) that "if the benevolent and Worthy are not trusted, the state will be empty and vacuous." More importantly, he also opined that "if someone honors the Worthy, employs the

43

capable, and has men of surpassing wisdom hold all the positions, throughout the realm men of talent will be pleased and willing to serve in his court."

The *Six Secret Teachings* preserves a succinct characterization of the differences between the modes of action identifiable with Sages and Worthies: "Sages concentrate on tranquilizing the people, Worthies focus on rectifying them." However, the most extensive differentiation was offered by Hsün-tzu, who divided men into five basic classes:

The Ordinary Man: His mouth cannot speak good words, his mind does not know modesty nor does he know to select worthy men and excellent gentlemen and entrust himself to them and thus has endless worry. He does not know what aspects of behavior to focus upon and in stopping and acting does not know where to settle. In his daily selection of things, he does not know what to value but follows them as if flowing along, not knowing where to return. His five emotions dictate, his mind follows and is destroyed.

The Gentleman: Although incapable of fully exhausting the techniques of the Tao, he will certainly accord with them. Even though he is incapable of excellence and goodness in all aspects, he will certainly dwell among them. Accordingly, in his knowledge he doesn't strive for extensiveness but concentrates upon thoroughly examining what he knows. In speech he does not strive for verbosity but concentrates upon examining what is discussed. And in his behavior he does not undertake too much but focuses on thoroughly examining the basis. Thus when his knowledge has solidified, his words convey the discussion, and his actions stem from proper motives, they will be as unchangeable as human nature, fate, and one's skin. Riches and nobility will be inadequate to increase him, poverty and lowliness insufficient to reduce him.

The Perfected Man: His words are loyal and trustworthy, but his mind does not regard this as virtuous. He embodies righteousness and benevolence, but his appearance does not boast of it. His thoughts and contemplations are enlightened and penetrating, but his language is not contentious, so it seems he can still be reached.

The Worthy: Their actions always accord with proper standards without suffering any injury to their original basis. Their words are sufficient to be taken as a model for All under Heaven yet are not detrimental to themselves. Even if they possessed the entire realm, they would not accumulate personal wealth; even though their generosity gave everything to the realm, they would not be troubled by poverty.

The Great Sage: His wisdom penetrates the Great Tao, he responds to change without being impoverished and is discriminating about the nature of the myriad things. The Great Tao is the means to change and transform the myriad things, while their nature is the means to impose patterns on taking or leaving. For this reason his affairs are pervasively discriminated amid Heaven and Earth, clearly investigated in the sun and moon. He unifies the myriad things in the wind and rain. Mysterious and ineffable, his affairs cannot be compassed. Just like the mastery of Heaven, his actions cannot be discerned, and in their ignorance the common people do not recognize his proximity.

Although probably highly congruent with Li's own views, these are of course the rather idealized and artificial definitions of a dedicated Confucian rather than a Taoist or Legalist.

Employing Worthies was therefore generally recognized by many as the most productive means for achieving greatness. Thus in his "Superior Strategy," Huang-shih Kung proclaimed: "The Tao for governing the state is to rely on Worthies and the people. If you trust the Worthy as if they were your belly and heart and employ the people as if they were your four limbs, all your plans will be accomplished." He also added: "Where the Worthy go they have no enemies before them," and noted (in "Inferior Strategy") that "the government of a Worthy causes men to submit with their bodies, the government of a Sage causes men to submit with their minds. When their bodies submit, the beginning can be planned, when their minds submit, the end can be preserved."

Even the draconian *Wei Liao-tzu* asserted in "Combat Awesomeness" that "if you raise the Worthy and give responsibility to the capable, even without the time being propitious, affairs will still be advantageous." If prosperity were to be achieved without conducting aggressive campaigns, Worthies need be acquired — essentially stolen — from other states: "To look at other peoples' lands and gain them, to divide up other rulers' subjects and nourish them, one must be able to absorb their Worthies. If you are unable to bring in and employ their Worthies but want to possess All under Heaven, you must destroy armies and slay generals. In this way, even though you may be victorious in battle, the state will grow increasingly weak. Even though you gain territory, the state will be increasingly impoverished."

As "knowing men" became a skill in itself, astute practitioners gained considerable fame for having been able to discern latent talent in demeaning positions, including men serving as cooks and butchers, just as noted in Li's narrative. Wisdom and clarity were known to be required, and several writers railed against relying on the opinion or judgment of others, particularly members of the court, because clandestine cliques and subversive collusion could severely distort any perception of actuality. Even Mencius warned (in IB7) that basing evaluations on public opinion could only prove erroneous, and the *Six Secret Teachings* includes a chapter entitled "Advancing the Worthy," which outlines the adverse consequences of relying on popular opinion:

> If the ruler takes those that the world commonly praises as being Worthies and those that they condemn as being worthless, the larger cliques will advance and the smaller ones will retreat. In this situation groups of evil individuals will associate together to obscure the Worthy. Loyal subordinates will die even though innocent and perverse subordinates will obtain rank and position through empty fame. In this way

turbulence will continue to grow in the world, and the state will not be able to avoid danger and destruction.

Apart from emphasizing the need for perspicaciousness, the *Liu-t'ao*'s "Honoring the Worthy" outlines what are termed "six thieves" and "seven harms." The former encompass deleterious behavior witnessed in court officials, the latter several manifestations that give the appearance of exceptionality but are fraudulent. To take but two examples:

Third, they make their appearance simple, wear ugly clothes, speak about actionless action in order to seek fame, and talk about nondesire in order to gain profit. They are artificial men, and the king should be careful not to bring them near. Fourth, they wear strange caps and belts, and their clothes are overflowing. They listen widely to the disputations of others and speak speciously about unrealistic ideas, displaying them as a sort of personal adornment. They dwell in poverty and live in tranquility, deprecating the customs of the world. They are cunning people, and the king should be careful not to favor them.

The ability to fabricate deceptive appearances would necessitate the development of methods and tests for evaluating men, for fathoming their true nature, of the sort that Li discusses in "Mirroring Talent."

MINOR JOTTINGS

A discussion of the origins and methods of "knowing men" may be found in the dedicated section by that name in my *The Tao of Spycraft*.

As advised by Shang Yang (in the first paragraph) and generally embraced by Li Ch'üan, rewards and punishments are fundamental. Accordingly, Li examines their nature and efficaciousness in a later chapter, "Punishments and Rewards."

Even though Wu Tzu-hsü was an exile, he managed to become King Ho-lü's security advisor prior to Sun-tzu's reported arrival and was responsible for formulating the strategy that allowed Wu to vanquish its nemesis Ch'u. Wu briefly became virtual hegemon until Yüeh, under Kou-chien, extinguished them after King Fu-ch'ai failed to heed Wu Tzu-hsü's warnings and admonitions. Fan Li, also mentioned in this chapter, played a somewhat similar role in Yüeh and supposedly composed a military text that disappeared early on except for scattered pronouncements.

7

將 有 智 謀

"GENERALS OF WISDOM AND STRATEGY"

The classics state that at the beginning of far antiquity, from Po Huang Shih down to Jung Ch'eng Shih, without issuing orders the people were transformed, without imposing punishments the people were ordered, and without bestowing rewards the people were motivated. Knowing neither anger nor happiness, they were as placid as infants. Pao Hsi Shih and Shen Nung Shih instructed but did not execute; Hsüan Yüan Shih (the Yellow Emperor), T'ao T'ang Shih, and Yu Yü Shih [of the Hsia] imposed executions, but no one was resentful.

Thus the three August Ones governed through the Tao and the Five Emperors through Virtue. When the Hsia, Shang, and Chou declined, the Spring and Autumn and Warring States abandoned the Tao and *Te* and relied instead upon wisdom and strategy. Ch'in relied upon Shang Yang and Li Ssu's wisdom to annex the feudal lords; Han employed Chang Liang and Ch'en

P'ing's wisdom to exterminate Hsiang [Yü's] clan; Emperor Kuang-wu employed Kou Hsün and Feng Yi's wisdom to bring about Fan Ch'ung's surrender; Ts'ao Ts'ao relied upon Hsü Yu and Ts'ao Jen's wisdom to destroy Yüan Shao. Sun Ch'ün relied upon Chou Yü and Lu Hsiao's wisdom to defeat Wei Wu; Liu Pei relied upon K'ung-ming's (Chu-ko Liang's) wisdom and became king of Western Shu; Chin relied upon Tu Yü and Wang Chün's wisdom to pacify Wu; Fu Chien relied upon Wang Meng's wisdom and settled the masses of the eight directions; Shih Leh relied upon Chang Pin's wisdom and captured Wang Chün alive; the T'uo-pa relied upon Ts'ui Hao's wisdom to preserve their armies north of the Yellow River; Yü Wen relied on Li Mu's wisdom to blunt Kao Huan's fierceness; the Liang relied upon Wang Seng-pien's wisdom to exterminate Hou Ching; the Sui relied upon Kao Chiung's wisdom and tied up Ch'en's ruler; and (T'ang) T'ai-tsung relied upon Li Ching's wisdom to defeat Chieh-li K'o-han.

No one who has ever possessed a state became king without relying upon wisdom and strategy. Thus it is said that the general is responsible for rectifying the governing principles in tranquility, employing spirit to investigate the subtle, and establishing things through wisdom. Perceiving good fortune within repeated tribulations and pondering misfortune that may lie beyond the depths of the darkness relies upon the general's wisdom and strategy.

SAWYER

Contrary to most analysts worldwide, rather than stressing courage or arraying a slew of essential abilities and crucial personality traits, Li initiates his examination of generals in the *T'ai-pai Yin-ching* simply with wisdom. However, his emphasis well accords with the impetus provided by the *Art of War*, which similarly gave priority to wisdom and thereby determined the orientation of discussions ever after even though the scope would quickly broaden to encompass a constellation of virtues, including courage. (Even Li's chapter 24, "Mirroring Talent," while pondering the broad topic of skill and the nature of officials, rather than being confined to commanders, still emphasizes wisdom and courage.)

Even though neophytes would continue to be entrusted with command because of their relationship with the ruler or their reputations, the increasing lethality of late Spring and Autumn warfare demanded the appointment of professional generals who had to be accorded independent authority once commissioned and dispatched into the field. Consequently, their abilities and characteristics, including wisdom, courage, and loyalty, immediately became crucial factors in the state's survival. According to the *Wei Liao-tzu*:

> When the commanding general takes up the drum, brandishes the drumsticks, and approaches danger for a decisive battle so that the soldiers meet and the naked blades clash, if he drums the advance and they respond to wrest victory, he will be rewarded for his achievements and his fame will be established. If he drums the advance but they fail, he will die and the state will perish. For this reason survival and extinction, security and danger all lie at the end of the drumstick! How can one not value the general?

In "The King's Wings," the T'ai Kung reiterated that "whenever the army is mobilized, it takes the commanding general as its fate. Its fate thus lies in a penetrating understanding of all aspects, not clinging to one technique." Even earlier, in "Military Combat" Sun-tzu had already concluded that "a general who understands warfare (知 兵 之 將) is Master of Fate for the people, ruler of the state's security and endangerment." This elicited Li Ch'üan's comment that "the general has the authority to kill and attack, his awesomeness is wanted to repel the enemy, what the people's fate is bound up with, therefore the state's security or endangerment lie in this." Insofar as the fate of the nation depends entirely dependent upon the general's acumen, Li concludes his chapter by substantially reflecting Sun-tzu's grave concern (expressed in "Nine Changes") that commanders must be wise enough to analyze the situation and determine the prospects for victory and defeat: "The wise must contemplate the intermixture of gain and loss. If they discern advantage [in difficult situations], their efforts can be trusted. If they discern harm [in prospective advantage], difficulties can be resolved."

Although Li never iterates what he deems should be a commander's essential characteristics, his commentary in the *Art of War* indicates he accepted the summation found in "Initial Estimations" that "the general encompasses wisdom, credibility, benevolence, courage, and strictness." In "Nine Terrains" Sun-tzu then noted that generals need to be tranquil and obscure, upright and self-disciplined, and capable of stupefying the troops. Furthermore, they have to be capable of knowing the enemy and assessing their own strengths and weaknesses, no mean achievement, which elicits Li's comment that "victory and defeat are not settled when someone takes himself to be strong and does not assess the enemy." Finally, generals have to be sagacious enough

to direct spying activities, control agents, and penetrate the nine crucial operational principles, otherwise termed the "nine changes," as well as know their troops are capable of attacking the enemy and whether the enemy can be attacked.

Even though he does not explicitly employ them, Li Ch'üan would certainly have been thoroughly familiar with all the early formulations that appear in the classic Warring States military writings. For example, according to the T'ai Kung, "Generals have five critical talents: courage, wisdom, benevolence, trustworthiness, and loyalty. If he is courageous, he cannot be overwhelmed. If he is wise, he cannot be forced into turmoil. If he is benevolent, he will love his men. If he is trustworthy, he will not be deceitful. If he is loyal, he won't be of two minds." Although Sun Pin's work had been lost by Li's time, it might be noted that his five are somewhat different, being righteousness, benevolence, Virtue, credibility, and wisdom.

The *Wei Liao-tzu* notes that the commanding general "should be composed so that he cannot be stimulated to anger. He should be pure so that he cannot be inveigled by wealth." And the late *Three Strategies of Huang Shih-kung* cites a purportedly ancient book entitled the *Military Pronouncements* in its discussion:

> Now, the general is the fate of the state. If he is able to manage the army and attain victory, the state will be secure and settled. The *Military Pronouncements* states: "The general should be able to be pure; able to be quiet; able to be tranquil; able to be controlled; able to accept criticism; able to judge disputes; able to attract and employ men; able to select and accept advice; able to know the customs of states; able to map mountains and rivers; able to discern defiles and difficulty; and able to control military authority."

Obviously by the time of the *Three Strategies*, the general had to possess a wide range of specific abilities, have thorough knowledge of military measures and essential techniques, and encompass essential character traits in order to withstand the fluctuating complexities of warfare.

Flaws and weaknesses, whether immediately apparent or well concealed (including those that will be pondered in Li's "Techniques for Probing the Mind" and "Mirroring Talent"), were also deemed highly troubling because they could doom military campaigns from the outset. Sun-tzu did not enumerate any until his eighth chapter, "Nine Changes," where it is stated that "generals have five dangerous [traits]. One committed to dying can be slain. One committed to living can be captured. One [easily] angered and hasty [to act] can be insulted. One obsessed with being scrupulous and untainted can be shamed. One who loves the people can be troubled." Accordingly, he warned that "these five dangerous traits are excesses in a general, potential disaster for employing the army. The army's destruction and the general's death will invariably stem from these five, so they must be investigated."

It was well recognized that even the most idealized virtues, when extreme or unrestrained by compensatory aspects, might bring about disaster. However, one of the most complete analyses of character flaws is preserved in a chapter appropriately called "A Discussion of Generals" in the *Six Secret Teachings*:

> What are referred to as the ten errors are as follows: being courageous and treating death lightly; being hasty and impatient; being greedy and loving profit; being benevolent but unable to inflict suffering; being wise but afraid; being trustworthy and liking to trust others; being scrupulous and incorruptible but not loving men; being wise but indecisive; being resolute and self-reliant; and being fearful while liking to entrust responsibility to other men.
>
> One who is courageous and treats death lightly can be destroyed by violence. One who is hasty and impatient can be destroyed by persistence. One who is greedy and loves profit can be bribed. One who is benevolent but unable to inflict suffering can be worn down. One who is wise but fearful can be distressed. One who is trustworthy and likes to trust others can be deceived. One who is scrupulous and incorruptible but doesn't love men can be insulted. One who is wise but indecisive can be suddenly attacked. One who is resolute and self-reliant can be confounded by events. One who is fearful and likes to entrust responsibility to others can be tricked.

Because flaws can be manipulated to secure military advantage, their recognition and exploitation became a conscious intelligence objective as early as the Warring States period. Thus in "The Tao of the General," Wu Ch'i advised:

> In general the essentials of battle are as follows: you must first attempt to divine the enemy's general and evaluate his talent. In accord with the situation, exploit the strategic imbalance of power for then you will not labor but still achieve results. A commanding general who is stupid and trusting can be deceived and entrapped. One who is greedy and unconcerned about reputation can be given gifts and bribed. One who easily changes his mind and lacks real plans can be labored and distressed.

Although he rarely speaks of command deficiencies in the *T'ai-pai Yin-ching*, his commentary to the *Art of War* indicates that Li was well aware of their potentially adverse impact. For example, he notes that "when the general's talent is not complete, the army will invariably be weak" and, in the case of one who loves the people, "attack what he loves for then he must roll up his armor and rescue them. When someone loves his people, you can plan to exhaust him." Moreover, he cites the interesting example of Chao She, who had surpassing book knowledge but neither the experience nor the wisdom to undertake military command. His appointment as commanding general, accomplished through Ch'in's employment of double agents in Chao's court, resulted in the debacle at Ch'ang-p'ing in 260 BCE in which Ch'in vanquished Chao's beleaguered forces and reportedly slew four hundred thousand prisoners. In contrast, Li obviously viewed Han Hsin's strategic acumen with great approbation because he cites his deliberate manipulation of Ch'ao's forces, his luring them forward for a decisive clash by casting his significantly outnumbered men onto fatal terrain beside a river, more than once in his commentaries and the *T'ai-pai Yin-ching*.

MINOR JOTTINGS:

In the *Military Methods*, Sun Pin identifies numerous command flaws (including being arrogant, greedy, indecisive, selfish, and fearful) and discusses their exploitation.

A discussion of Han Hsin's repeated exploitation of unorthodox measures, all of which remain subjects of contemporary study, may be found in my *Tao of Deception*.

8

術 有 陰 謀

"TECHNIQUES INCLUDE CLANDESTINE PLANS"

The classics state that "those in antiquity who excelled in employing the military invariably placed great emphasis upon the tactical balance of power (*ch'üan*) prevailing throughout the realm and thoroughly investigated the strategies of the feudal lords. If the tactical imbalance of power is not thoroughly investigated, lightness and weightiness, strength and weakness will not be known. If the nature of things is not thoroughly assessed, the movement and stillness of hidden changes and concealed transformations will not be known. In weighing tactical imbalance, nothing is more difficult than achieving comprehensive knowledge, in assessing nothing harder than ferreting everything out, and in military affairs nothing more difficult than achieving certain success. The worthy rely on these three.

Thus techniques for achieving a hundred victories in a hundred conflicts do not realize the pinnacle of excellence for they are not as good as subjugating the enemy's forces without engaging in combat, the very pinnacle of excellence. The most skillful employ strategic plans, the next human affairs, the lowest warfare and assaults. Those who employ strategic plans dazzle and mystify the enemy's ruler. They secretly dispatch sycophantic ministers to trouble his affairs; they befuddle him with shamans and sorcerers, resulting in him esteeming ghosts and spirits. They cause colorful garb and embroidered clothes to be valued, prompting beans and grain to be disdained and his storehouses and granaries to be empty. They dispatch beautiful women and superlative things in order to mesmerize his will and send skilled carpenters in order to encourage him to undertake palaces and high towers, thereby exhausting the state's wealth and expending its strength. They change his nature, transforming him to licentiousness, extravagance and brutality, arrogance and dissipation. Worthy men then bite their tongues, no one being willing to correct or help him.

When he promiscuously rewards and wantonly punishes in accord with his own happiness and anger, governmental orders are no longer implemented; he believes in submitting to indications provided by ghosts and spirits; quashes the loyal but advances sycophants; and personal requests are publicly enacted, no worthy men will participate in the government.

[It soon happens that] he awards offices to those he loves, grants rank to men without achievement, rewards those who have not labored, pardons criminals when he is happy but uses the laws to slay when he is angry. Although ordinances have been established, he acts willfully; orders are issued but not implemented; and he believes in [divination] by milfoil stalks, turtle plastrons, and other means. Ghosts and spirits, priests and ritualists, sycophants and flatterers, practitioners of unorthodox skills, and strange goods chaotically circulate within his gate. Everything that he refers to as "correct" is [actually] wrong, everything he terms "wrong" is actually correct.

Separate the ruler from his ministers, impede the path of loyal remonstrance. Thereafter debauch him with beauty, assault him with profit, mislead him with pleasure, nurture him [with unusual] tastes. Cause him to take good faith to be deceit and deceit to be good faith, loyalty to be betrayal and betrayal to be loyalty. When the loyal remonstrators have all perished and sycophants and flatters are being rewarded, you will have brought it about that perfected men [chün-tzu] dwell in the wilds while menial men occupy official positions. Orders might be urgently issued and brutal actions undertaken, but the people will be unable to bear the burden.

This is what is referred to as subverting the enemy through clandestine strategies without engaging in combat because his state is already destroyed. If you follow up with troops, the ruler can be captured, his state toppled, his cities seized, and his masses shattered. Thus when King T'ang employed this method, King Chieh of the Hsia was displaced; when the Chou used it, Emperor Hsin [of the Shang] was slain; when Yüeh employed it, Wu was turned into a wasteland; when Ch'u employed it, Ch'en and Ts'ai arose; when the three important families employed it, Lu was weakened; and when Han and Wei employed it, the Eastern Chou was split.

Pedestrian thinkers all say that strong, large armies will invariably be victorious while small weak ones will certainly perish. If this were true, no rulers from minor states would have ever achieved the greatness of hegemony nor would any ruler with ten thousand chariots have ever suffered the balefulness of destruction. In antiquity the Hsia was expansive and Shang limited, then the Shang was great and the Chou small, and finally Yüeh was weak and Wu strong. What is referred to as conquering without engaging in combat, the strategy of clandestine toppling, and the Tao of nighttime activities results from teaching both the civil and martial. Isn't it true that only the worthy can perceive and take pleasure in this?

SAWYER

When penning his chapter on subversive techniques, a method esteemed for achieving victory with minimal or no fighting, Li

Ch'üan was able to contemplate three lengthy articulations that dated back many centuries: "Civil Offensive," "Three Doubts," and Wen Chung's multistep program. (The first two, both found in the *Six Secret Teachings*, would be much condemned in the Sung and thereafter for their purported perversity and extreme divergence from the path of Virtue. Wen Chung's integrated measures for toppling the state of Wu at the end of the Spring and Autumn is retrospectively—and thus no doubt imaginatively—chronicled in the seminovelistic *Wu-Yüeh Ch'un-ch'iu*.) In bemoaning the ruler's loss of control, chapters in the classic military writings (such as "Superior Strategy" in the *Three Strategies*) and Han Fei-tzu's "Eight Villainies") also describe court behavior symptomatic of decline and show how rulers can be corrupted and manipulated by their subordinates, thereby indirectly suggesting measures that might be employed to achieve similar results in more ordered states.

"Civil Offensive" is purportedly predicated upon the historically poignant situation in which the subservient state of Chou sought to overturn the repressive and tyrannical Shang, an objective dramatically accomplished in the decisive battle at Mu-yeh. However, throughout history these principles have been understood as applicable in any two-party relationship, though especially when one of the members is decidedly inferior in strength or position. Extensively abridged, the chapter runs:

First, accord with what he likes in order to accommodate his wishes.

Second, become familiar with those he loves in order to fragment his awesomeness.

Third, covertly bribe his assistants, fostering a deep relationship with them.

Fourth, assist him in his licentiousness and indulgence in music in order to dissipate his will. Make him generous gifts of pearls and jade and ply him with beautiful women. Speak deferentially, listen respectfully, follow his commands, and accord with him in everything.

Fifth, treat his loyal officials very generously but reduce the gifts you provide to the ruler. Delay his emissaries, do not listen to their missions. When he eventually dispatches other men, treat them with sincerity, embrace and trust them.

Sixth, make secret alliances with his favored ministers but visibly keep his less favored outside officials at a distance.

Seventh, if you want to bind his heart to you, you must offer generous presents. To gather in his assistants, loyal associates, and loved ones you must secretly show them the gains they can realize by colluding with you.

Eighth, gift him with great treasures and make plans with him.

Ninth, honor him with praise. Do nothing that will cause him personal discomfort. Display the proper respect accruing to a great power, and your obedience will certainly be trusted. Magnify his honor, being the first to gloriously praise him, humbly embellishing him as a Sage.

Tenth, be submissive so that he will trust you and thereby learn about his true situation. Accept his ideas and respond to his affairs as if you were twins.

Eleventh, block up his access by means of the Tao. Among subordinates there is no one who does not value rank and wealth nor hate danger and misfortune. Secretly express great respect toward them and gradually bestow valuable gifts in order to gather in the more outstanding talents.

Twelfth, support his dissolute officials in order to confuse him. Introduce beautiful women and licentious sounds in order to befuddle him. Send him outstanding dogs and horses in order to tire him. From time to time, allow him great power in order to entice him to greater arrogance.

Although each of the measures is specifically correlated with expected results, the focal objective is isolating, debauching, and thoroughly manipulating the ruler in order to enervate his state and destroy its chance for survival.

"Three Doubts," albeit similarly couched in terms of the much-maligned Shang, expounds the preferred method for undermining enemy rulers:

> In order to attack the strong, you must nurture them to make them even stronger and increase them to make them even more extensive. What is too strong will certainly break, what is too extended must have deficiencies. Attack the strong through their strength. Cause the estrangement of their favored officials by using their favorites and disperse their people by means of the people.
>
> You should become involved with [the ruler] in numerous affairs and ply him with temptations of profit. Conflict will then surely arise.
>
> If you want to cause his close supporters to become estranged from him, you must do it by using what they love, making gifts to those he favors, giving them what they want. Tempt them with what they find profitable, thereby making them ambitious. Those who covet profits will be extremely happy at the prospects, and their remaining doubts will be ended.
>
> Now, without doubt the Tao for attacking is to first obfuscate the king's clarity and then attack his strength, destroying his greatness and eliminating the misfortune of the people. Debauch him with beautiful women, entice him with profit. Nurture him with flavors and provide him with the company of female musicians. Then after you have caused his subordinates to become estranged from him, you must cause the people to grow distant from him while never letting him know your plans. Appear to support him and draw him into your trap. Don't let him become aware of what is happening, for only then can your plan be successful.

The fourth paragraph of "Civil Offensive" and the last paragraph just above clearly advocate one of China's favored measures for weakening opponents, whether enemy states or barbarian kingdoms: entice the ruler and his key advisors with the allure of beauty and debauch them with scents, music, and sexual delights. This will not only cause the state's resources to be uselessly expended and inveigle the ruler into neglecting the government but also ensure that critics, however moderate, and remonstrators will be viewed as troublesome annoyances and brusquely dismissed, if not executed.

Li Ch'üan would have been thoroughly cognizant of another diabolical program historically associated with the death struggle that developed between King Fu-ch'ai of Wu and King Kou-chien of Yüeh. (As it is fully described in our *Tao of Spycraft*, only crucial aspects need be noted here.) As a result of foolishly attacking the state of Wu, King Kou-chien had been reduced to a small enclave, completely dependent upon Wu's suffrage for their continued existence. Dedicating himself to reviving Yüeh and gaining revenge, for five years he enacted programs designed to enrich the state before starting to systematically implement the measures intended formulated by Wen Chung to subvert his enemy. The most important of Wen's recommendations included:

> First, revere Heaven and serve ghosts in order to seek their blessings. Second, make generous presents and monetary gifts to the ruler and numerous presents and bribes to please his ministers. ...Fourth, present the ruler with beautiful women in order to befuddle his mind and confuse his plans.... Fifth, send the ruler skilled artisans and excellent materials to stimulate him to undertake palaces and mansions and thereby exhaust their wealth... Sixth, dispatch sycophantic ministers, causing the ruler to become easily attacked. Seventh, stiffen those ministers who dare to remonstrate, forcing them to commit suicide.

Specific actions were formulated to successfully enact each measure. For example, to realize the fifth, "send the ruler skilled artisans and excellent materials to stimulate him to undertake palaces and mansions and thereby exhaust their wealth," Wen Chung advised that "some sacred materials should be selected from the famous mountains and presented to the king." (Wen had observed that Fu-ch'ai "loves to erect palaces and mansions and employs his workers without respite.") Despite protests that taking advantage of those superlative materials would exhaust the people, Fu-ch'ai employed them to erect a grand tower. The efforts required eventually resulted in "men dying on the roads and the sound of wailing and crying being unbroken in the lanes and alleys. The people were exhausted and the officials embittered, men had nothing by which to live."

Thereafter in order to take advantage of the simplest but historically most effective means for befuddling enemies, Yüeh presented him with two surpassing beauties. They not only succeeded in totally mesmerizing the king but also further estranged him from his perspicacious security advisor, Wu Tzu-hsü. Thereafter the state of Wu was brought to the tipping point by the first historically known biologically based ploy when Yüeh repaid the grain they had previously borrowed to rescue the people from (a feigned) famine with seeds that had been heated and would no longer germinate. Starvation and misery resulted when Wu employed it throughout their domain, radically weakening the state and making it vulnerable to invasion.

Wen Chung's program had become well-known long before the T'ang. Some bureaucratic thinkers, just as Wen Chung previously, claimed that ancient rulers, including King T'ang of the Shang and King Wu of the Chou, two paragons of virtue in imperial-era portraits of events, had employed them. However, following Mencius others vehemently insisted that such despicable actions would not even have been conceivable and tried to quash discussions about them because their mere contemplation contravened state efforts to promote Virtue and morality.

9

術 有 探 心

"TECHNIQUES FOR PROBING THE MIND"

In antiquity neighboring states could see each other's signal fires and hear the sounds of each other's chickens and dogs, but their footsteps never met within the borders of the feudal lords nor did the tracks of their wagons intersect more than a thousand *li* away. They preserved life through the Tao, tranquilized their bodies with Virtue, and the people took pleasure in their dwellings. Later, when the winds of degeneracy arose, purity and simplicity dispersed. Authority and wisdom were employed, prevarication and artifice were born. Neighboring states used spies in their intercourse with each other, the vertical and horizontal alliances employed forceful persuaders. The state of Hsü cleaved to benevolence and righteousness, but its altars were laid waste, the state of Lu esteemed Confucianism and Mohism, but their ancestral temples were destroyed.

Unless you penetrate the mysterious and know the subtle, you will not be able to resist your enemies. Unless you exert your mind and trouble your thoughts, you will not be able to penetrate the source of affairs. Unless you can always distinguish the real and false, you will not be able to achieve fame. If you are not perspicacious about talent, you will not be able to employ the military. If you cannot discern loyalty and disloyalty, you will never be able to judge men. For this reason Master Kuei-ku secretly composed four chapters — "Pai-ho," "Ch'uai-mo," "Fei-ch'ien," and "Ti-hsi" — to instruct the famous Warring States strategists Su Ch'in and Chang Yi, who then wandered among the six states and probed the minds of the feudal lords, after which his techniques were practiced.

In general, to employ the techniques of mental probing begin by intermixing and inclusively speaking about the Tao, Virtue, benevolence, righteousness, the rites, music, loyalty, trust, the *Book of Odes*, the *Book of Documents*, the *Tso Chuan*, the philosophers, histories, plots and stratagems, success and failure. Settle the subject's mind, tranquilize his intentions, spy out his emotions, what he loves and hates, likes and dislikes, and employ his desires to attack him. Secretly ponder but outwardly express something different in order to approach him with specious words while he responds sincerely. Then compare his mind and his appearance, listen to his sounds and investigate his words. If his speech does not cohere with them, turn about and seek out the truth. When he has been forced to truly respond and you have fathomed his mind, turn again to strike at his meaning. If his responses have no gap, if they cohere tightly, then bind him closely, do not let him reverse anything, just the way Yang Yu grasped his bow or Feng Meng took up an arrow and never missed in a hundred shots. It is just like setting out traps to net fish or rabbits, catching their mouths, restraining their waists, and compressing their ribs. [Once they have been trapped], even though they bang about, they merely get hung up in the netting and none escape.

Now, to probe the mind of the benevolent you must employ sincerity, not wealth. To probe the heart of a courageous warrior you must employ righteousness, not fear. To probe the mind of a wise officer you must employ loyalty, not deceit. To probe the mind of a stupid man you must use obscurity, not brightness. To probe the mind of a menial man you must employ fear, not the ordinary. To probe the mind of the greedy you must employ bribes, not integrity.

Now, when you speak with the wise, you should rely on erudition because wisdom has limits while erudition has none. Therefore the wise will not be able to fathom such breadth.

When you speak with the erudite, rely upon disputation. The erudite take antiquity as their teachers, but disputation responds to the present, so the erudite are unable to respond to such facileness.

When you speak with the noble, rely upon political power, for although the noble have high position, they are controlled through power. Even position cannot stop power.

When you speak with the rich, rely upon things. The rich accumulate wealth, but there are treasures that even their wealth proves inadequate to acquire.

When you speak with the poor, rely upon profits. The poor suffer from want and impoverishment while great profits can provide abundant aid. The impoverished lack the means to provide aid of any magnitude.

When you speak with the lowly, rely upon deference because the lowly rank below other men, as the term asserts. By being deferential they cannot then speak about humbleness.

When you speak with the courageous, rely upon daring because the courageous dare to be firm and resolute. Then the courageous will not be able to monopolize firmness.

When you speak with the stupid, rely upon sharpness because the stupid are simple and substantial while sharpness is brilliant and enlightened. Then the stupid will not be able to investigate the intelligent.

These eight are all founded upon their similarity in the Tao but differ in their final expression. By employing the Tao of what people want to hear but making the end expression different, they will listen but fail to understand. In this way they will be unable to fathom shallowness or depth. When they are unable to fathom shallowness or depth, I will be able to go out where there is no chink and enter where there is no gate. I can go alone and come alone, sometimes horizontally, sometimes vertically. This can be compared [to the wind] bending dry grass over—if blowing eastward, it bends east, if westward, it bends west—or like stopping up a river's current so that when the dam is broken it flows but when obstructed ceases. What worry is there that plans will not be followed?

Now, the Tao esteems controlling men, not being controlled by men. Those who control others take hold of authority, those who are controlled by others comply with their commands. The technique for controlling others is to avoid their strengths and attack their weaknesses while displaying your own strength and concealing your shortcomings. Thus when animals move, they first strike with their claws and teeth, when birds move, they will invariably employ their beaks and talons, when insects and snakes move, they will always employ poison, and when shelled creatures move, they use their shells [for protection]. Since birds, animals, insects, and snakes all employ their strength to wrest control over other animals, how much more so will the wise?

People who like to discuss the Tao and Virtue must be broken with benevolence and righteousness. Those who like to speak about the ways of Confucianism and Mohism must be controlled with the theories of the horizontal and vertical alliances. Those who like to speak about laws and regulations must be repressed with techniques and authority. You must contravene their beginnings, accord with their conclusions, destroy their teeth, and knock their horns off, never letting them escape your control. Thereafter gradually speak about either gleeful or depressing affairs to make them happy or trouble their hearts, causing their spirits to be unable to act as masters of their minds.

Discussions focused on longevity, tranquility, pleasure, riches, nobility, honor, glory, music, and sex are joyful. Death, perishing, depression, misfortune, poverty, mean condition, bitterness, insults, punishment, execution, and fines all involve words concerned with mourning. When you speak to the noble with such words of mourning, they will grieve, while if you speak to the lowly about gleeful affairs, they will be pleased. Take command of their minds, respond to their thoughts, sometimes joyously, sometimes mournfully, in order to befuddle their intentions. When their emotions change within, their appearance will alter without. Constantly observe their external manifestations in order to discern the concealed. This is termed the technique for fathoming the hidden and probing the mind. Even the Tao of the former kings, the methods of the Sages and the Wise, are inadequate for achieving hegemony over the realm without this technique.

SAWYER

In this chapter Li Ch'üan focuses upon verbally confounding others in structured interviews designed to probe their minds and discover intent. Moreover, he even speaks about employing these methods to stupefy the people, much in accord with a thought tendency that advocated keeping the people ignorant. Thus he states: "By employing the Tao of what people want to hear but making the end expression different, even though they listen, they will fail to understand. In this fashion they are unable to fathom the shallow or deep. Thus I am able to go out where there is no chink and enter where there is no gate. I can go alone and come alone, sometimes horizontally, sometimes vertically."

Although, as mentioned in the section on "Honoring the Worthy," "knowing men" had become a crucial skill and matter of great import to the state by the end of the Spring and Autumn period, and several Warring States political thinkers and military writers developed fairly comprehensive reality tests that will be discussed in the commentary to chapter 24, "Mirroring Talent." However, in attempting to fathom men, their emphasis tended to be on personality and characteristics with a secondary focus on penetrating discrepancies between manifest behavior and actual substance. Only *Han Fei-tzu* and *Kuei-ku Tzu* pondered words and their implications, the former primarily in a chapter titled

"Difficulties of Persuasion" that discusses numerous methods and techniques for exploiting human tendencies and personality traits in order to effectively persuade others to change their thinking or adopt a desired course.

While clearly reflecting lessons and techniques explicated in the *Han Fei-tzu*, Li's approach is much more aggressive, unrelenting, and even brutal because he assaults his target both directly and indirectly in order to simultaneously fathom and convert, to structure and control. Moreover, he largely adopts the approach, language, and techniques found in the first section of the *Kuei-ku Tzu*, especially the chapters titled "Pai-ho," "Fan-ying," "Nei-chieh," and "Ti-hsi." However, he is less concerned with orienting in terms of yin and yang and more focused on "opening and closing," verbally contorting and then discerning gaps and fissures that can be exploited. Both works discuss eight subject categories, but in "Ch'üan" Kuei-ku Tzu investigates whether people are Worthies or not, wise or stupid, courageous or fearful, and benevolent and righteous.

Of course, a ruler seeking to control others in this fashion would violate all the actionless precepts advanced by Han Fei-tzu and others, especially the more fundamental proponents of Taoism who would certainly be sorely troubled. Thus it is somewhat surprising that he discordantly asserts that "the Tao esteems controlling men, not being controlled by men. Those who control others take hold of authority, those who are controlled by others comply with their commands." However, although similar statements appear in several of the classic military writings, it is quoted exact from "Mou" ("Plans") in the *Kuei-ku Tzu*.

"Techniques for Probing the Mind" opens by again noting that many adverse changes have beset the human realm and recognizing that society has deteriorated from enjoying innocence and adhering to Virtue to practicing deceit, duplicity, and mayhem. Li actually begins by essentially drawing upon the image conveyed by the concluding lines of a *Tao Te Ching* chapter titled "A Small State with Few People":

Given a small state with few people —
Cause them to have military organizations of ten and a hundred,
But not employ them,
And ensure the people value their deaths and not travel far off.
Even though they have boats and wagons, they will then have no place to ride them,
Even though they have armor and weapons, they will then have no place to deploy them.
Bring it about that the people revert to knotting ropes and using them,
Make their food sweet,
Beautify their clothes,
Provide stability to their dwellings,
And make their customs pleasurable.
Then, although neighboring states look across at each other,
And the sounds of roosters and dogs be mutually heard,
Unto old age and death, the people will not travel back and forth.

This devolution accounts for the somewhat surprising deprecation of Confucianism and Mohism, their teachings having become inadequate to preserve states in an environment in which power and authority prevailed.

MINOR JOTTINGS

Although the extant *Kuei-ku Tzu* includes all four chapter titles Li Ch'üan cites, rather than captioning a single segment, "Ch'uai-mo" is actually split into two, "Ch'uai" and "Mo."

10

政 有 誅 強

"THE GOVERNMENT EXECUTES THE STRONG"

The classics state that when a state has those who cause disorder within the army, the officers and troops will become fearful and weak, the implements and weapons soft and blunted, orders issues by the government fragmented, and rewards and punishments unclear.

Those who bring about disorder in the army include wealthy aristocrats, powerful ministers, palace attendants, and various favorites. When they hold military rank, they affect the army's strategic power and encroach upon the commanding general's awesomeness. Public government is then manipulated by private interests, and private households drain the public treasury. Superiors issue plans, but subordinates block them with discussions; superiors promulgate orders, but inferiors do not implement them. Some (troops) are as fierce as tigers, others as fearful as sheep. Some are cruel as wolves, others so strong that they cannot be controlled. This is what is meant by a turbulent army. They should all be executed.

King Wen Hsüan (Confucius) executed Shao-cheng Mao between two gate towers, and the state of Lu was quieted; Ssu-ma Jang-chü beheaded Chuang Chia beneath the camp gnomon, and all within the army became solemn; Wei Chuang-tzu exterminated Yang Kan, and the feudal lords all submitted; and Hsiang Yü beheaded Sung Yi, and all under Heaven were terrified. Executing the wealthy augments your awesomeness, exterminating the strong augments your authority. Awesomeness and authority are given birth from the bodies of the wealthy and strong, not from ordinary officers and obtuse troops.

If there are any men who have multiple talents among the wealthy and strong, then harness and control them, instruct and lead them just like training birds of prey or raising fierce animals. You must first moderate their eating and drinking, clip their claws and teeth, fetter their feet, and secure their tongues so that they come when you call and race off when you signal. Cage and imprison their hearts, make them follow closely whether you go left or right. However, increase the perversity of the wealthy and strong who lack multiple talents, let them accumulate their villainy, give rein to their wills and extend their intentions so that the misfortune spreads throughout the Three Armies. When enmity has been brought about throughout the army and you execute them, it will magnify your *ch'i*.

Thus it is said that the evil are materials for the good. Generals are responsible for leading the state's armies. If they do not execute the wealthy and strong, how can they create the requisite awesomeness?

SAWYER

Creating the charisma and awesomeness necessary to command men and ensure obedience has always been a pivotal military issue. Long before Li Ch'üan composed this chapter, the classic military writers and other political thinkers of the Warring States period realized that rampant exceptionalism invariably subverts authority. In his "Superior Strategy," Huang-shih Kung astutely cited some preexistent observations on this problem:

> The *Military Pronouncements* states: "When the branches [the ruler's relatives] and leaves [the powerful families] are strong and large, forming parties and occupying positions of authority so that the lowly and mean insult the honored and they grow more powerful with the passing of time while the ruler cannot bear to dismiss them, the state will suffer defeat from it."
>
> The *Military Pronouncements* states: "When deceitful ministers hold superior positions, the entire army will be clamoring and contentious. They rely on their awesomeness to grant personal favors and act in a manner that offends the masses. Advancement and dismissal lack any basis, the evil are not dismissed, and men seek gain with any appearance possible. They monopolize appointments for themselves and in advancements and dismissals boast of their own merits. They slander and vilify those of great Virtue and make false accusations against the meritorious. Whether good or evil, all are treated the same. They gather and detain affairs of government so that commands and orders are not put into effect. They create a harsh administration, changing the ways of antiquity and altering what was common practice. When the ruler employs such wanton characters, he will certainly suffer disaster and calamity."

However, difficulties always entail opportunities, and it was quickly realized that dramatically excising powerful offenders would have far more psychological impact than punishing ordinary people. Conversely, conspicuously honoring the lowest ranks for their accomplishments emphasizes that rewards are not reserved for the mighty alone. Thus, according to "The General's Awesomeness" in the *Six Secret Teachings*:

> The general creates awesomeness by executing the great and becomes enlightened by rewarding the small. Prohibitions are made effective and laws implemented by careful scrutiny

in the use of punishments. Therefore, if by executing one man the entire army will quake, kill him. If by rewarding one man the masses will be pleased, reward him. In executing, value the great; in rewarding, value the small. When you kill the powerful and the honored, punishment reaches the pinnacle. When rewards extend down to the cowherds, grooms, and stablemen, rewards are penetrating downward to the lowest. When punishments reach the pinnacle and rewards penetrate to the lowest, then your awesomeness will have been established.

A similar passage preserved in the *Wei Liao-tzu*'s "Martial Plans" no doubt provides an indication of the view's widespread acceptance. Furthermore, the idea of augmenting strength until it breaks even appears in the *Tao Te Ching*'s "Wanting to Reduce Something":

> If you want to reduce something, you must certainly stretch it.
> If you want to weaken something, you must certainly strengthen it.
> If you want to abolish something, you must certainly make it flourish.

By allowing perversity free reign, the commander magnifies the impact of the moment of punishment. Not only does he thereby suppress the strong, but having overspread the army their perniciousness will have caused such annoyance and consternation that everyone will welcome their elimination.

In "Punishments and Rewards," Shang Yang notes that when Duke Wen of Chin, the earliest of the powerful Spring and Autumn hegemons, executed a highly favored individual in heinous fashion for arriving late at a conclave, all his officials trembled, and Chin subsequently enjoyed noticeable military success. However, it was the story of Ssu-ma Jang-chü beheading a great official in order to establish his awesomeness that obviously impressed Li Ch'üan because he cites it several times in the *T'ai-pai Yin-ching* and raises it as an example in his commentary to the *Art of War*:

Ssu-ma Jang-chü was a descendant of T'ien Wan. During the time of Duke Ching of Ch'i, Chin attacked [the major cities of] A and P'in, and Yen invaded [the river district] Ho-shang. Ch'i's army suffered a total defeat, sorely troubling Duke Ching. Yen Ying then recommended Jang-chü, saying: "Even though Jang-chü is descended from T'ien's concubine, in civil affairs he is still able to attach the masses and in martial affairs overawe the enemy. I would like my lord to test him." Duke Ching summoned Jang-chü and spoke with him about military affairs. He was greatly pleased and appointed him as general of the army to lead the soldiers in resisting the armies of Yen and Chin.

Jang-chü said, "Formerly I was lowly and menial. If my lord pulls me out from my village and places me above the high officials, the officers and troops will not be submissive, and the hundred surnames will not believe me. Since I am insignificant and my authority light, I would like to have one of my lord's favored ministers, someone whom the state respects, serve as supervisor of the army. Then it will be possible." Duke Ching assented and had Chuang Ku go forth.

Jang-chü, who had already taken his leave, made an agreement with Chuang Ku, saying: "Tomorrow, at midday, we shall meet at the army's gate." Jang-chü raced ahead to the army, set up the gnomon and let the water [drip in the water clock], awaiting Ku. Ku, who had always been arrogant and aristocratic, assumed that since the general had already reached the army while he was [only] the supervisor, it was not extremely urgent. Relatives from all about who had come to send him off detained him with drinking. Midday came and Ku had not arrived. Jang-chü then lay down the standard, stopped the dripping water, and went into [the encampment]. He advanced the army, took control of the soldiers, clearly publicizing the constraints and bonds. When the constraints had been imposed and it was already evening, Chuang Ku arrived.

Jang-chü asked: "How is it that you have arrived after the appointed time?"

Ku acknowledged his fault, saying, "High officials and relatives saw this simple one off, thus he was detained."

Jang-chü said: "On the day a general receives the mandate [of command], he forgets his home; when he enters the army and takes control of the soldiers, he forgets his loved ones; when he takes hold of the drumsticks and urgently beats the drum, he forgets himself.

"Enemy states have deeply invaded [our land], and there is unrest and movement within the state. Officers and soldiers lie brutally cut down and exposed at the borders. Our ruler does not sleep soundly or enjoy the sweet taste of his food. The fate of the hundred surnames hangs upon you, so what do you mean by being seen off?"

He summoned the provost marshal and inquired: "What are the army's rescripts regarding those who arrive after the appointed time?" He replied: "They should be decapitated!"

Terrified, Chuang Ku ordered a man to race back and report to Duke Ching, asking that he be saved. He had already left but not yet returned when [Jang-chü] beheaded Ku in order to publicize [the enforcement of discipline] within the Three Armies. All the officers within the Three Armies shook with fear.

Li might have also used the (probably apocryphal) story of how Sun-tzu proved the efficacy of his organizational methods by melodramatically having two of King Ho-lü's concubines beheaded when they failed to obey his commands as part of a demonstration that employed three hundred palace women in the embattled state of Wu.

The symptoms that mark disordered and thus vulnerable, if not doomed, states recur in several classic military writings and Warring States political works such as the *Han Fei-tzu* even though their focus was primarily directed to court officials. Although Li Ch'üan sometimes decries the inescapable necessity to employ rewards and punishments and writes almost wistfully of eras in which Virtue's prevalence made them irrelevant, he realistically accepted the need for their implementation and thus discusses them in several contexts, including here and in the aptly titled "Punishments and Rewards."

MINOR JOTTINGS:

The incident from Ssu-ma Jang-chü's life appears in his biography in the *Shih Chi*.

11

善 師

"EXCELLING IN COMMAND"

The classics state that in employing the military the perfected man [*chün-tzu*] would not employ anything other than the Tao, Virtue [*Te*], benevolence, and righteousness even though he might become hegemon over All under Heaven.

Beginning with Duke Yin of Lu when the Tao of the Chou had already declined, the feudal lords began to create their own rites and music and usurped the right to conduct expeditions and assaults. Ch'i mounted sudden strikes on the strong with their skillful fighters, Wei arose through the use of highly martial troops, and Ch'in gained victory through elite warriors. Disputants made Sun-tzu and Wu-tzu their foundation, only Hsün Ch'ing (Hsün-tzu) spoke about the Tao of true kingship and criticized them.

[In his "Discussion of the Martial," Hsün-tzu] said that "Ch'i's skillful raiders were the troops of a lost state, Wei's

81

martial troops those of an endangered state, Ch'in's elite warriors composed an army striving for rewards and treading in profit, and that only the armies of Duke Huan of Ch'i and Duke Wen of Chin can be said to have invaded others and remain organized and constrained." Accordingly, [Hsün-tzu asserted that] "Ch'i's mercenary raiders could not have withstood Wei's martial troops; Wei's martial troops would not have been a match for Ch'in's elite fighters; Ch'in's elite fighters could never have opposed the well-ordered troops of Duke Huan; and Duke Huan's well-organized armies could not have opposed T'ang and Wu's benevolence and righteousness."

Thus it is said that those who excel in command never deploy; those who excel in deployments never engage in battle; those who excel in battle are never defeated; and those who excel at defeat never perish. Solitary and alone, the Yellow Emperor stood in the center [of the world] and was victorious over the four emperors. This is what by those who excel in command do not deploy into formation.

King T'ang and King Wu conducted punitive attacks, deployed their forces, issued oaths to the masses, and then went on to depose Chieh of the Hsia and capture Chou [Hsin] of the Shang. This is what is meant by those who excel in deployments never engage in battle.

In the south Duke Huan [of Ch'i] caused strong Ch'u to submit and make contributions to the Chou house, in the north he attacked the Shan Jung (mountain barbarians) and opened a path to Yen. This is what is meant by those who excel in battle are never defeated.

King Chao of Ch'u suffered misfortune at the hands of King Ho-lü [of Wu], his state was extinguished and he fled, racing with his brothers to beseech Ch'in for aid. Ch'in sent their troops forth, and the king of Ch'u was able to return to his state. This is what is meant by those who excel at defeat do not perish.

Now, the army is the means by which to preserve the lost, continue the severed, rescue the chaotic, and eliminate harm. Through Yi Yin's and Lü Shang's (T'ai Kung's) generalship, their own descendants continued to possess their states right through the end of the Shang and Chou dynasties. But when deceit, strength, avarice, and brutality came to prevail in later ages, the disciples of Sun-tzu, Wu-tzu, Han Fei-tzu, and Pai Ch'i were all executed and their posterity cut off.

Now, "weapons are inauspicious implements, warfare is a dangerous affair." However, clandestine (yin) plans contravene Virtue and result in employing baleful implements. Therefore, without Tao and *Te*, loyalty and trust one cannot settle the disasters affecting the realm nor eliminate the harm being suffered by the masses of humanity.

SAWYER

Although Li Ch'üan clearly believes that Virtue and righteousness are fundamental to the state and its survival, he found himself grudgingly compelled to recognize that the times had changed, that society had deteriorated from the ideal age when Virtue prevailed, making warfare inescapable. Thus, as already noted, he vacillates between accepting the inescapable need to employ force and asserting the ultimate superiority of Virtue and righteousness. Ultimately, as he asserts in the concluding paragraph, subterfuge and clandestine methods (as well as brute force and aggressive attacks) are necessary but being inherently dangerous and inimical can only be properly implemented by men of Virtue.

Several Warring States writings propounded the idea that warfare is ultimately perverse and that weapons are dangerous implements that should normally be kept stored away, preferably unused. (Li again gives voice to this view early in the next chapter, "Esteeming Harmony," and in his commentary to the *Art of War* in which he notes that "the *Ch'un Ch'iu* states that weapons are like fire. If they are not stored away, they will consume themselves.") However, the quintessential expression is found in the *Tao Te Ching*, particularly the first three lines of "Superlative Weapons":

> Superlative weapons being inauspicious implements,
> There are things that detest them.

Thus, those that attain the Tao do not dwell among them.

Another chapter, "Assisting the Ruler with the Tao," speaks of the inimical results:

> One who assists the ruler with the Tao
> Does not coerce the realm with weapons.
> Such affairs easily rebound.
> Wherever the army has encamped,
> Thorny brambles will grow.
> After large armies have flourished,
> There will certainly be baleful years.

Despite bemoaning the brutal and wasteful nature of warfare and recognizing the suffering and ruin that follow in its wake, much in accord with Li Ch'üan's statement that "the army is the means by which to preserve the lost, continue the severed, rescue the chaotic, and eliminate harm," the classic military writings still posited it as necessary. Thus, in "Audience with King Wei," Sun Pin reportedly said: "Victory in warfare is the means by which to preserve vanquished states and continue severed generations. Not being victorious in warfare is the means by which to diminish territory and endanger the altars of state. For this reason military affairs cannot but be investigated."

In his chapter on military affairs, Hsün-tzu stated that the righteous man engages in warfare to end violence and eliminate harm, not to strive for acquisition. However, the "classic" assertion appears in the *Ssu-ma Fa*'s "Benevolence the Foundation":

> In antiquity, taking benevolence as the foundation and employing righteousness to govern constituted uprightness. However, when uprightness failed to attain the desired objectives, [they resorted to] authority (*ch'üan*). Authority comes from warfare, not from harmony among men. For this reason if one must kill people to give peace

to the people, then killing is permissible. If one must attack a state out of love for their people, then attacking it is permissible. If one must stop war with war, although it is war it is permissible. Thus benevolence is loved; righteousness is willingly submitted to; wisdom is relied upon; courage is embraced; and credibility is trusted. Within, [the government] gains the love of the people, the means by which it can be preserved. Outside, it acquires awesomeness, the means by which it can wage war.

Remarkably, even Shang Yang and the *Tao Te Ching*'s authors reluctantly came to the same conclusion. "Superlative Weapons" continues:

> Weapons are inauspicious implements,
> Not the instruments of the perfected man.
> But when he has no alternative but to employ them,
> He esteems calmness and equanimity.
> Victories achieved are not glorified,
> For glorifying them is to take pleasure in killing men.
> One who takes pleasure in killing men
> Cannot achieve his ambitions under Heaven.
> Auspicious affairs esteem the left,
> Inauspicious affairs esteem the right.
> Subordinate generals occupy the left,
> Commanding generals the right.
> This states that one treats military affairs as rites of mourning.
> After killing masses of the enemy's men,
> Weep for them with grief and sorrow.
> After being victorious in battle,
> Implement the rites of mourning.

Conversely, although many envisioned a need for warfare and defensive preparations, Sun-tzu warned against prolonged engagements, and several other ancient authors equally cautioned against becoming enthralled with warfare or employing it for expansionistic purposes. Thus, in "Audience with King Wei," Sun Pin asserted that "one who takes pleasure in the military will perish, and one who finds profit in victory will be insulted. The military is not something to take pleasure in, victory is not something through which to profit." Similarly, in "Benevolence the Foundation," the *Ssu-ma Fa* proclaimed that "even though a state may be vast, those who love warfare will inevitably perish. Even though calm may prevail under Heaven, those who forget warfare will certainly be endangered." Even the comparatively draconian *Wei Liao-tzu* notes in "Army Orders, I" that "weapons are inauspicious instruments, conflict is a contrary virtue. All affairs must have their foundation. Therefore, when a true king attacks the brutal and chaotic, he takes benevolence and righteousness as the foundation."

The idea not just of regionalism but of locally determined behavioral traits and tendencies defined in part by personality and ethical concerns recurs in this chapter. Li's focus falls upon a hierarchical ranking determined by their Virtue and righteousness, those more closely adhering to ideal ways invariably subjugating those of lesser virtue. As background, the series of characterizations and the correlated tactics that might be employed to defeat states with such attributes now found preserved in the *Wu-tzu* might be noted:

> Although Ch'i's battle arrays are dense in number, they are not solid. Those of Ch'in are dispersed, and their soldiers prefer to fight individually. Ch'u's formations have good order, but they cannot maintain their positions for long. Yen's formations are adept at defense, but they are not mobile. The battle arrays of the Three Chin are well controlled, but they prove useless.
>
> Now, Ch'i's character is hard, the country prosperous, and the ruler and ministers arrogant, extravagant, and insulting to the common people. The government is expansive, but salaries are inequitable. Every formation is of two minds, with the front being heavy and the rear light. Thus while they are dense, they are not stable. The Tao for attacking them is to

86

divide them into three and then harry and pursue the left and right, coercing and following them, for then their formations can be destroyed.

Ch'in's character is strong, the land treacherous, and the government severe. Their rewards and punishments are believed, the people never yield but instead are all fiery and contentious. Thus they scatter and individually engage in combat. The Tao for attacking them is to first entice them with profits because their soldiers are greedy and will abandon their generals to pursue them. Capitalizing on their misjudgments, you can hunt down their scattered ranks, establish ambushes, take advantage of the moment, and capture their generals.

Ch'u's character is weak, the lands broad, the government troubling [to the people], and the people weary. Thus while they are well-ordered, they do not maintain their positions for long. The Tao for attacking them is to suddenly strike and cause chaos in the encampments. First snatch away their *ch'i*, lightly advancing and then quickly retreating, tiring and laboring them, never actually joining battle. Then their army can be defeated.

Yen's character is sincere and straightforward. Its people are careful, they love courage and righteousness, and rarely practice deception in their plans. Thus they will defend their positions but are not mobile. The Tao for attacking them is to strike and press them, insult them and put distance between you, then race and get behind them so that their upper ranks will be doubtful and their lower ranks fearful. Be cautious about your chariots and cavalry, avoiding conflict on the open road, and then their general can be captured.

The Three Chin are central countries. Their character is harmonious and their government equitable. The populace is weary from battle but experienced in arms, and they have little regard for their generals. Salaries are meager, and as their officers have no commitment to fight to the death, they are ordered but useless. The Tao for attacking them is to press [points in] their formations and oppose them when large numbers appear. When they turn back, pursue them in order to wear them out. That then is the strategic configuration of power in these countries.

Although all the states in Wu-tzu's enumeration suffer exploitable defects, Li Ch'üan definitely reserved his greatest approbation for Hsün-tzu's conquest hierarchy.

12

貴 和

"ESTEEMING HARMONY"

The classics state that in the Tao of the former kings, harmony was esteemed. When this esteem for harmony was emphasized, the people did not incline to warfare. The *Tso Chuan* states: "If the ruler treats the feudal lords with Virtue, who among them will dare not submit; if the ruler coerces the feudal lords with force, who among the them will willingly submit in their hearts?"

The state of Ch'u had square fortifications about their capital and regarded the Han River as their pool. Nevertheless, even though their troops were numerous, they were useless. For this reason Duke Tao of Chin had Wei Chiang establish harmonious relationships with the Jung in order to rectify the numerous Hua clans. In eight years he held nine conclaves of the feudal lords that might be compared to the harmonious playing of music free of any discordant notes, and even the Ch'iang gave their allegiance. Duke Hui accepted them as subjects who would neither encroach upon nor rebel against Chin, and they subsequently furnished components for the army that fought at Yao Pass [against Ch'in]. It might be compared with catching a deer, with Chin seizing the antlers and the men of Jung grabbing the legs.

Rulers who have penetrated the Tao are able to subjugate others through Virtue. Benevolent rulers are able to harmonize people with righteousness; wise rulers are able to gain victory over others through strength; rulers who rely upon authority are able to control men through power. Gaining victory through combat is easy, through harmony difficult. The *Kuo Yü* states that "the former kings flourished Virtue and never displayed their weapons (army) so that when the army was assembled and moved in accord with the need of the moment, it was awesome. When weapons are displayed, they will be treated as playthings; when they are treated as playthings, they will not inspire trembling. Thus they held formal conclaves but not convocations for making covenants; they held warlike assemblies but never got caught up in combat and deployment."

Weapons are inauspicious implements that should be employed only when unavoidable. This is why the emperors and former kings of far antiquity conquered others when they mobilized their armies, and their achievements surpassed the masses. First they embraced them with the civil (文) and Virtue, but if they did not submit proffered gifts of jade and silk in order to entice them. If they could not entice them into coming, they ordered their commanding generals to train charioteers and horses, sharpen their elite soldiers, and [as Sun-tzu states in the *Art of War*], "Attack where they are unprepared, go forth where they will not expect it." This is what is meant by necessarily extirpating the rebellious but invariably being lenient with the submissive. After they had embraced and been generous toward them, they could display their Virtue.

The *Shang Shu* [*Book of Documents*] states, "When instructing them, employ attractive means, when supervising them, employ awesomeness." When it was thus, then even the four Yi [eastern tribal peoples] did not pose any obstacle to unification nor was it necessary to worry about bringing the Eight Jung to court.

SAWYER

"Kuei Ho" purportedly stresses the idea of harmony yet readily admits that "gaining victory through combat is easy, through harmony difficult." Moreover, Li still recognizes warfare's necessity, albeit framed in terms of its inimical nature and the primacy of Virtue. The text also betrays a certain arrogance in assuming the existence of a proper world order and unquestioningly believing that the great leaders of antiquity had an innate right to subjugate others, especially external (or so-called "barbarian") peoples who are normally condemned for failing to acknowledge the Heavenly sanctioned claims of the Hsia, Shang, and Chou dynasties.

The classic military writers discuss cohesiveness in terms of "unity" (*t'ung* 同) and "harmony" (*ho* 和). The former might be achieved through such coercive measures as rewards and punishments, but in the view of many theorists, including the Confucians, their employment will not result in the proper volitional component, the essential foundation of "harmony." Nevertheless, everyone agreed that unity and harmony were necessary for states to prosper and successfully engage in warfare, and harmony was posited as one of the crucial foundations of strength. However, simply employing benign measures in the hope of achieving harmony throughout the realm, although considered ideal, was deprecated by some thinkers as unlikely to succeed because Virtue, righteousness, and benevolence had been, and could be, simply brushed aside by those with perverse values and inimical objectives. (As already noted, Wu Ch'i and others, including Li himself, were painfully aware that several states had been extinguished despite cultivating Virtue.)

Harmony's importance is most famously expounded in *Mencius* (IIB1): "The seasons (*shih/shi* 時) of Heaven are not as good as advantages of Earth; advantages of Earth are not as good as harmony among men." Mencius even provided a (badly flawed) martial example for contemplation:

Suppose a city with an inner wall three *li* in circumference and an outer wall of seven is encircled and assaulted, but the attackers are not victorious. In order to encircle and assault it, they must have gained the moment of Heaven, but they were not victorious because the moments of Heaven are not as good as advantages of Earth. However, in cases where the walls were high, the moats deep, their weapons and armor sharp and sturdy, millet and corn plentiful but they were coerced into abandoning it and fleeing, it is because advantages of Earth are not as good as harmony among men.

The saying about the seasons of Heaven certainly predates Mencius and is widely found in both political and military writings, including the *Wei Liao-tzu* ("Combat Awesomeness"), where it is understood simply as stressing the need for human effort. Despite debunking beliefs in Heavenly influences, in the next chapter, Li still asserts that "armies not modeled on Heaven should not act, those not patterned on Earth should not move, punitive expeditions and attacks not in harmony with men should not be brought to completion. Heaven must sanction the time, Earth make its resources available, and men define the plans." Moreover, in his *Art of War* commentary, he concludes, "When human affairs, the seasons of Heaven, and advantages of Earth, all three, are known, then a hundred victories will be achieved in a hundred engagements."

Rather than just harmony, the military writings tend to speak about both. In "Initial Estimations" the *Art of War* asserts that "the Tao causes the people to be fully in accord with the ruler. They will die with him, they will live with him and not fear danger." Despite its penchant for individuality, the *Huai-nan Tzu* similarly stressed the idea of unity in military contexts, and the *Wei Liao-tzu* observed that "those who are unified will be victorious, those beset by dissension will be defeated." However, it would be Wu Ch'i who astutely characterized the dynamics:

In antiquity those who planned government affairs would invariably first instruct the hundred surnames and gain the affection of the common people.

There are four disharmonies. If there is disharmony in the state, you cannot put the army into the field. If there is disharmony within the army, you cannot deploy into formations. If you lack harmony within the formations, you cannot advance into battle. If you lack cohesion during the conduct of the battle, you cannot score a decisive victory.

For this reason when a ruler who has comprehended the Tao is about to employ his people, he will first bring them into harmony and only thereafter embark on great affairs. He will not dare rely solely upon his own plans but will certainly announce them formally in the ancestral temple, divine their prospects by the great tortoise shell, and seek their confirmation in the Heavens and seasons. Only if they are all auspicious will he proceed to mobilize the army.

Both civil and military methods are to be employed, the former primarily entailing instruction, governmental policies, ritual, and laws, the latter consisting of strict organization and military training, especially drilling, and battlefield measures such as making the drums, flags, and signal fires numerous, just as advised in the *Art of War*'s "Military Combat" and generally followed thereafter. It was commonly said that the troops had to become as responsive to the commander's intent as if they were his four limbs, no mean feat since they were also supposed to be kept ignorant of it.

MINOR JOTTINGS:

The last paragraph of Wu Ch'i's program provides an interesting vestige of earlier thought and practices because he advises seeking the sanctification of the ancestors in the state temple and turning to prognostication rather than relying solely upon human-based assessments to determine the advisability of undertaking an expeditionary campaign.

13

廟 勝

"VICTORY IN THE TEMPLE"

The classics state that Heaven esteems preserving the full and adhering to the patterns of yin and yang and the four seasons. Earth esteems stabilizing the precarious and observing the individuality of life and what is appropriate to ordinary land. Men esteem constraint in affairs, the harmonization of yin and yang, and the publication of seasonal edicts. When affairs come, they respond to them, when things come, they know them. All under Heaven fully exhaust their loyalty and good faith and follow the government's orders. Thus it is said [in the *Six Secret Teachings*] that "when the Tao of Heaven is free of disasters, you cannot come before them; when the Tao of Earth lacks calamities, you cannot take the lead; when human affairs have not suffered any losses, you cannot attack first."

The four seasons encroaching upon each other; deluge and drought increasing and receding; thunder occurring in the winter and frost in the summer; and flying insects devouring the fields are all disasters of Heaven.

Landslides in the mountains and rivers congealing; seeds not germinating in the earth; water not irrigating the ground; the five grains not ripening and the eight cereals not maturing are all calamities of Earth.

Heavy taxes and onerous government, high towers and deep pools; excessive labor mobilization; drunkenness, orgies, and licentiousness; loyal officials estranged and sycophants favored; soldiers exhausted and the army spent through prolonged employment are all losses in the human realm.

. In this way Heavenly disasters are discerned above, calamities of Earth are observed below, and human losses witnessed all about.

Armies not modeled on Heaven should not act, those not patterned on Earth should not move, punitive expeditions and attacks not in harmony with men should not be brought to completion. Heaven must sanction the time, Earth make its resources available, and men define the plans. When the enemy is quiet, observe their yang [visible] aspects, when they move, investigate their yin [hidden] side. First observe their traces, thereafter know the enemy's mind.

What is termed a victorious army is victorious first and then seeks to engage in battle, whereas a defeated army first engages in battle and then seeks victory. Thus [in "Military Disposition" Sun-tzu] said: "Before the engagement one who determines in the ancestral temple that he will be victorious has found that the majority of factors are in his favor. Before the engagement one who determines in the ancestral temple that he will not be victorious has found few factors are in his favor. If one who finds that the majority of factors favor him will be victorious while one who has found few factors favor him will be defeated, what about someone who finds no factors in his favor? Observing it from this perspective, victory and defeat will be apparent."

SAWYER

The *Art of War* was the first Chinese military work to broach the idea of employing calculation to accurately determine the possibilities of victory before engaging in warfare. Although a fundamental advance in rationalizing military science, it equally reflected Sun-tzu's focus on the human realm and his commitment to excluding spiritual and superstitious influences from the decision making process. "Victory in the Temple" opens by apparently contemplating nonhuman influences, but Li Ch'üan redefines the important indications visible in the three realms of Heaven, Earth, and Man in terms of natural phenomena, including disasters, and chooses "symptoms" that reflect classic concerns with benevolent government, economic prosperity, and programs that neither impoverish nor exhaust the people. (The early writers, including Hsün-tzu, Shang Yang, Han Fei-tzu, and the authors of the *Six Secret Teachings* and other classic martial writings, provide numerous characterizations of inimical symptoms or encroachments and ill behavior that adversely impact the quality of government.)

This naturalistic interpretation thus underpins his paraphrase of a passage found in the *Six Secret Teachings* that originally discussed whether the appropriate moment had dawned for the Chou to revolt against the Shang. According to "Opening Instructions," "If there are no ill omens in the Tao of Heaven, you cannot initiate the movement to revolt. If there are no misfortunes in the Tao of Man, your planning cannot precede them." Moreover, the thrust to accurately evaluating the enemy encapsulated by Li's admonition that "when the enemy is quiet, observe their yang [visible] aspects, when they move, investigate their yin [hidden] side. First observe their traces, thereafter know the enemy's mind" similarly echoes a passage from "Opening Instructions" in the *Six Secret Teachings*: "You must look at the Shang king's yang aspects and moreover his yin side for only then will you know his mind. You must look at his external activities and also his internal ones for only then will you know his thoughts."

Having been composed in an era of increasingly lethal strife when a single misstep could doom a state to extinction, the *Art of War* chose to emphasize the crucial nature of warfare by opening with the statement that "warfare is the greatest affair of state, the basis of life and death, the Tao for survival or extinction. It must be thoroughly pondered and analyzed." Thereafter, throughout the book, rationality, self-control, and the need to avoid engagements not based upon detailed analyses of the situation, including combat options and the army's capabilities, are stressed. Commanders must be as knowledgeable about themselves as the enemy, a requirement succinctly expressed by the famous utterance that "in warfare, those who know the enemy and know themselves will not be endangered in a hundred engagements. Those who do not know the enemy but know themselves will sometimes be victorious, sometimes meet with defeat. Those who know neither the enemy nor themselves will invariably be defeated in every engagement."

Prior to mobilizing for a campaign, detailed calculations should be performed in the ancestral temple and similar, presumably more specific assessments, initiated by the commander before engaging an enemy force in the field. Although undertaken in the ancestral temple for ritual and psychological reasons, they were not a form of divination (such as mentioned by Wu-tzu in my comments to the previous chapter) but instead an early form of net assessment based upon quantified estimates that systematically assigned numerical values to the strength of objectively determined factors for both sides. Five parameters are identified in "Initial Estimations":

> Which ruler has the Tao?
> Which general has greater ability?
> Who has gained [the advantages of] Heaven and Earth?
> Whose laws and orders are more thoroughly implemented?
> Whose forces are stronger?
> Whose officers and troops are better trained?
> Whose rewards and punishments are clearer?
> From these I will know victory and defeat.

Although these five factors were deemed fundamental, the *Art of War* identifies an additional forty paired, mutually defined, interrelated categories that might be employed to undertake assessments. These include Heaven/Earth, hunger/satiety, exhausted/rested, ordered/disordered, fearful/confident, cold/warm, wet/dry, and lax/alert. If the results prove positive, "after assessing the advantages in accord with what you have heard, put them into effect with strategic power supplemented by field tactics that respond to external factors."

Conversely, if the enemy enjoys an insurmountable advantage, warfare should not be initiated. Similarly, commanders in the field who find themselves confronting a superior force must either avoid it, assume a defensive posture, or conceive and implement tactics that will negate the enemy's superiority and expose his weaknesses. Rather than an extemporaneous enterprise stimulated by foolhardy desire or prompted by volatile emotion, warfare would thus be converted into an art or science. The *Art of War* therefore offered the conclusion Li cites in closing the chapter.

Highly impressed by Sun-tzu's conception, Li Ch'üan appended a very lengthy comment to the *Art of War* passage:

Those who excel in warfare contend for advantage with others only after determining through temple calculations that they will be successful. Attacking the rebellious and embracing the distant, toppling the lost and solidifying the extant, and uniting the weak and attacking the benighted are all manifestations. The interior and exterior becoming estranged, as in the case of the Shang and Chou armies, is what is referred to as having determined victory through temple calculations before engaging in combat. According to the *T'ai-yi Tun-chia* assessment method, any score above sixty is considered a majority (*tuo suan*), anything below sixty a minority. When a guest [invader] with a majority score approaches a defender [host] with a minority score, the host will be defeated. But if a guest with a minority score engages someone with a majority, then the host will be victorious. In all these cases, victory and defeat are easily seen.

However, in the broader context of the *Art of War*'s thought, it was not merely victory, or even one hundred victories in one hundred engagements, that was being sought, but conquering without any fighting at all. Moreover, as the *Art of War* asserts, warfare should not be initiated out of personal desire, anger, or a quest for revenge but only to ensure the state's survival. However, while basically concurring, Li would certainly add achieving the properly glorious objectives of enlightened rule.

14

沉 謀

"SUBMERGED PLANS"

The classics state that those who excelled at employing the army could not have established themselves without trust and righteousness, achieved victory without yin and yang, deployed without the unorthodox and orthodox, nor engaged in battle without deceit and subterfuge.

Plans are concealed in the mind, but affairs are visible in external traces. One whose thoughts and visible expression are identical will be defeated, one whose thoughts and visible expression differ will be victorious. Thus [Sun-tzu said], "Warfare is the Tao of deception. When capable, display incapability. When about to employ the army, feign that you are not."

When your mind is filled with great plans, display only minor concerns. When your mind is planning to seize something, feign being about to give it away. Obscure the real, cast suspicion upon the doubtful. When the real and doubtful are not distinguishable, strength and weakness will be indeterminable.

Be profound like the Mysterious Origin free of all images, be an abyss like the unfathomable depths of the sea. When you attain this, yin and yang can no longer be employed to calculate your intentions, ghosts and spirits will be unable to know them, techniques and measures unable to impoverish them, and divinatory methods unable to fathom them, so how much more so enemy generals!

Now, those who excelled in warfare achieved their victories in the clash of armies. The historical records are inadequate to attest to their plans, the form of their victories too insubstantial to be observed. Those who can discuss tactics but not implement them harm a state while those who can implement them but are unable to discuss them can be employed by the state. Thus it is said, "The highest plans are not spoken about, great military affairs are not discussed." It is subtle and mysterious!

Thus outstanding generals are able to penetrate the patterns of Heaven and Earth and fully comprehend the nature of the myriad things. They profit the greedy, thereby nurturing their desires, and are deferential to the strong, making them arrogant and boastful. They estrange the intimate, causing them to become mutually disaffected. Men with insatiable desires will lack uprightness, the arrogant and boastful will neglect their defenses, and disaffected strategists will depart.

King Wen of the Chou made generous gifts to the Shang, and the Shang king was subsequently slain. King Kou-chien of Yüeh humbled himself before the state of Wu, and King Fu-ch'ai of Wu was eventually exterminated. Han Kao-tsu became estranged from the kingdom of Ch'u, and Hsiang Yü, king of Ch'u, perished. Thus one subjugates the feudal lords with words and labors the feudal lords with plans.

Those who excel in commanding the army attack what the enemy loves so that they must respond and strikes their vacuities so that the enemy must follow. They multiply their methods to coerce the enemy into dividing and fabricate suspicious activities to force the enemy to prepare. When the enemy is responding and following, they will be unable to defend their cities. When they have to divide and prepare, they will be unable to unite their soldiers. Thus we will be rested while they are labored, they will be few while we are many.

Attacking the tired with the rested accords with martial principles, attacking the rested with the tired contravenes martial principles. Attacking the few with the many is the Tao for military victory, attacking the many with the few is the Tao for military defeat. Attacking the few with the many and assaulting the tired with the rested is the way to attain complete victory.

Debilitating the enemy's spirit, seizing the general's mind, exhausting the strength of their troops, and severing thousand-*li* supply routes do not lie in martial force or in the strategic power of deployments effected by stalwart warriors but in wise officers calculating the tactical imbalance of power (*ch'üan*). It is weak and soft! Roll it up, it won't fill the space of a sleeve. It is deep and secretive! Stretch it out, it will surpass the seas.

A five-inch bolt can control the opening and closing of a door, a square inch of mind can change success to defeat. Thoroughly knowing all the aspects of the myriad things and thus never being imperiled, flexibly completing the myriad things without omitting any, according with Heaven and trusting men, investigating the beginning and knowing the end, what worry is there that one's plans will not be followed?

SAWYER

"Submerged Plans" is the only *T'ai-pai Yin-ching* chapter that mentions fundamental tactical principles. All of them are either direct quotations or paraphrases from the *Art of War* and primarily focused upon defeating the enemy as efficiently as possible through manipulation, deceit, and the unorthodox. However, although the chapter still incorporates the customary appeal to Virtue, the first part emphasizes the importance of being unfathomable. Only then will it be possible to shape the enemy's actions while nurturing a sort of defensive invulnerability.

The need for secrecy is a frequent behest in the classic military writings. For example, in "Military Discussions" the *Wei Liao-tzu* noted that "control of the army is as secretive as the (depths of) Earth, as dark and obscure as the (heights of) Heaven, and is given birth from the nonexistent." Similarly, in a quintessential *Six Secret Teachings* passage from "The Army's Strategic Power," the T'ai Kung stressed the importance of secrecy:

> Strategic power is exercised in accord with the enemy's movements. Changes stem from the confrontation between the two armies. Unorthodox and orthodox tactics are produced from the inexhaustible resources [of the mind]. Thus the greatest affairs are not discussed, and the employment of troops is not spoken about. Moreover, words that discuss ultimate affairs are not worth listening to, the employment of troops is not so definitive as to be visible. They go suddenly, they come suddenly. Only someone who can exercise sole control, without being governed by other men, is a military weapon.
>
> If [your plans] are heard about, the enemy will make counter plans. If you are perceived, they will plot against you. If you are known, they will put you in difficulty. If you are fathomed, they will endanger you.

Secrecy being an unexpectedly complex issue, disagreement arose how best to preserve it. Unimaginative writers were satisfied with mundane measures such as reminding the troops to keep silent about military plans, implementing techniques intended to secure encampments against both external agents and internal defectors, and requiring commanders to wait until the moment for action before unveiling their tactics and objectives. However, far more sophisticated approaches ranging from simple concealment through misdirection and deliberately stupefying the troops were also advocated to achieve the pinnacle of being unfathomable.

Within this context the chief debate was over whether it was better to be deceptive or formless. The former has the collateral benefit that the enemy might be manipulated to good advantage, the latter (as expressed in Sun-tzu's conception in "Vacuity and Substance") ensures not just being unknowable but also causing the enemy to disperse their forces and prepare against all eventualities and induces paralyzing doubt. As the second paragraph notes, behavior and expression readily betray the most secret plans; nevertheless, in Li's opinion being mysterious and formless surpasses deception in concealing the real and mystifying the enemy.

The military discussion ("Ping-lüeh-hsün") included in the *Huai-nan Tzu* (which actually denies that employing the worthy will lead to victory) contains the most developed articulation of formlessness in terms already familiar from the contents of the *T'ai-pai Yin-ching*:

Among the spiritual nothing is more honored than Heaven, among strategic power nothing more conducive than earth, among movements nothing more urgent than time, and among employments nothing more advantageous than man. These four are the trunk and branches of the army, but they must rely upon the Tao before they can be implemented and attain unified employment.

Advantages of earth overcome seasons of Heaven, skillful attacks overcome advantages of earth, and strategic power conquers men. Those who rely on Heaven can be confused, who rely on earth can be constrained, who rely on time can be pressed, and who rely on men can be deluded.

Benevolence, courage, trust, and purity are attractive human attributes, but the courageous can be enticed, the benevolent can be seized, the trusting can be deceived, and the pure are easily plotted against. If the army's commander displays any one of these attributes, he will be captured. From this perspective it is clear that armies control victory through the patterns of the Tao, not through relying upon the talents of worthies.

Only those without form cannot be ensnared. For this reason the Sage conceals himself in the originless so that his emotions cannot be perceived. He moves in the formless so that his deployments cannot be fathomed. Without tactics or appearance, he acts appropriately. Without name or shape, he changes and creates an image. Even among those with acute vision, who can spy out his nature?

From Sun-tzu's bold pronouncement that "warfare is the Tao of deception" onward, deceit and deception have remained core concepts in Chinese military science. Although the subject is far too extensive to pursue here, it should be noted that the *Art of War* also initiated recognition of the various possibilities by outlining several basic measures: "Although [you are] capable, display incapability to them. When committed to employing your forces, feign inactivity. When [your objective] is nearby, make it appear as if distant; when far away, create the illusion of being nearby." Naturally they should all be employed to manipulate the enemy as part of the quest to enervate and disorder their forces, as well as compel them into disadvantageous circumstances in which the army's strategic power (*shih*) might be brought to bear.

One paragraph in "Submerged Plans" revisits the idea of employing the sort of subversive actions already discussed in "Techniques Include Clandestine Plans." Apart from his favorite example of King Kou-chien of Yüeh prevailing over Fu-ch'ai of Wu, (contrary to the image of Virtue conquering) Li somewhat surprisingly notes that King Wu allayed Emperor Hsin's suspicions with generous gifts. (Li's conclusion that "one subjugates the feudal lords with words and labors the feudal lords with plans" derives from "Nine Changes" in the *Art of War*.)

"Debilitating the enemy's spirit, seizing the general's mind, and exhausting the strength of their troops," three crucial techniques in the quest for victory, were all similarly first broached by the *Art of War*. Sun-tzu discusses waiting for the enemy's spirit to abate before drumming the attack, but he never intended that commanders should confine themselves to such simplistic, albeit insightful, measures. Instead they should physically enervate the enemy, sever their supplies, and generally implement any actions that might quash their fervor. Thereafter, well-rested forces are expected to easily dispatch now wearied and depressed opponents, thereby conforming to warfare's basic principles.

Apart from being another way of being formless, a deliberately fabricated appearance can provoke a desired response in the enemy. Thus Sun-tzu said that "one who excels at moving the enemy deploys in a configuration (*hsing* 形) to which the enemy must respond. He offers something that the enemy must seize. With profit he moves them, with the foundation he awaits them." However, as just noted an ancillary but still vital step was seizing the mind of the enemy commander, an objective first elucidated in "Military Combat." Neither Sun-tzu nor the *T'ai-pai Yin-ching* offer any specific suggestions for achieving this aim, but in his commentary to the *Art of War* Li mentions four techniques: "Anger him and cause him to be enraged, perturb him to cause him to be disordered, estrange him to cause him to be distanced, be humble to cause him to be arrogant." By the T'ang the art of exploiting flaws in enemy commanders, already visible in its inception in the *Art of War* and perhaps best epitomized by several chapters in Sun Pin's *Military Methods*, had extensively developed, with "seizing his mind" being just one of several objectives.

MINOR JOTTINGS:

Although Li never really discusses the nature of unorthodox warfare, several chapters refer to it and, in concord with Sun-tzu, who first articulated the concept, he clearly assumed that the successful practice of warfare required it. (For an extensive discussion, see my *Tao of Deception: Unorthodox Warfare in Historic and Modern China*.)

Sun-tzu's famous *ch'i* (qi 氣) passage appears in the *Art of War*'s chapter "Military Combat": "The *ch'i* of the Three Armies can be snatched away, the commanding general's mind can be seized. For this reason in the morning their *ch'i* is ardent; during the day their *ch'i* becomes indolent; at dusk their *ch'i* is exhausted. Therefore, one who excels at employing the army avoids their ardent *ch'i* and strikes when it is indolent or exhausted. This is the way to manipulate *ch'i*."

Sun-tzu may have gained this insight from a historically well-known Spring and Autumn battle now preserved in a *Tso Chuan* summary account: "During the Spring and Autumn period, the state of Ch'i attacked the state of Lü. Duke Chuang, commanding Lü's forces, was about to commit the army to battle when Ts'ao Kuei requested permission to join him. The Duke had him ride in his chariot and went into battle at Ch'ang-shao. The duke was about to have the drums sound the advance when Ts'ao Kuei said to him: 'Not yet.' Ch'i sounded their drums three times then Ts'ao said: 'Now.' They beat the drums, engaged in combat, and severely defeated Ch'i's army. The duke inquired why Ts'ao Kuei had delayed the drums. Ts'ao replied: 'Combat is a matter of courageous *ch'i*. A single drumming arouses the soldiers' *ch'i*, with a second it abates, and with a third it is exhausted. They were exhausted while we were vigorous, so we conquered them.'"

15

子 卒

"TROOPS"

The classics state that in antiquity they did not employ the people's strength for more than three days a year, and the portion of their harvest taken as taxes did not exceed one tenth. "[The predynastic Chou leader] Kung Liu liked material goods, so the inhabitants all had accumulations in their storehouses, and travelers had sacks of provisions. T'ai Wang [of the Chou] loved beauty (sex), so there were no frustrated women within the inner quarters of houses and no solitary bachelors without." King Wen created punishments, but the state did not unjustly imprison anyone. King Wu mobilized the army, and the warriors took pleasure in death.

In antiquity it never happened that those who excelled in leading men were able to employ their strength without first gaining their allegiance nor that they were able to gain their deaths without acquiring their strength. Thus states must establish the customary forms of behavior (*li*), fidelity, intimacy, and love before men will exchange hunger for surfeit. The customs of filiality, loving-kindness, integrity, and shame must prevail in the state before men exchange death for life. The reason that men will fight to the death in defense or attack is that their commanders treat them generously. When their commanders treat them generously, they respond fervently.

Neither the officers nor troops have any blood relationship or kinship with their commanding general, yet he can cause them to risk sharp edges and arrow points, rush against shields and blades, and die without turning about on their heels because he has nurtured them with beneficence and good faith, led them by customary ritual and compassion, and immersed them in small acts of kindness just the way a solicitous father loves his children. Thus they can escape from impending danger and extricate themselves from difficulties [such as posed by] mud and ashes.

[Superlative] commanders humble themselves before their warriors. They are united with them in sweetness and bitterness, personally look after those suffering from illness, do not wear fur robes in the cold nor use fans in the heat. They do not ride horses when ascending nor open umbrellas in the rain. When the army's tents have not yet been set out, generals do not speak about sitting, when the army's wells have not been dug, they do not speak about thirst. Their wives repair the officers' clothes while on campaign, they attribute credit for achievements to their subordinates. If they provide a cask of superlative wine, they will certainly dump it into the river. Their words of encouragement circulate among the army.

For this reason their men like to hear the sound of the metal blades clashing, and their courageous *ch'i* is aroused by the beating of the great and small drums [to advance]. It is not that they hate life and take pleasure in death but that they want to repay their generals with their lives. Thus [Sun-tzu] said, "If you regard the troops like children, you can go with them into the deepest valley. But if you regard them as beloved children, you can die with them. If you treat them generously but are unable to love them, or if you love them but are unable to give them orders, or if you are unable to discipline when they are unruly, just like a spoiled child they cannot be used." For this reason "commanding them with the civil and unifying them with the martial" is termed "being certain to seize." Another saying has it that "husbands and wives in harmony can attack Ch'i, even angry young men can attack Lu." Wang Chien, Li Mu, Wu Ch'i, and Ssu-ma Jang-chü all employed this technique, and their soldiers were the strongest among the feudal lords.

SAWYER

Somewhat contrary to its title, "Troops" actually focuses upon the complex issue of leadership, of gaining the allegiance of the troops and maintaining their commitment to their commander. Although Shang Yang and a few other early thinkers advocated relying solely upon punishments and rewards (as will be seen in the upcoming *T'ai-pai Yin-ching* section with that name), and Li sometimes veers toward accepting that belief, most of the military thinkers believed that acquiring the troops' willing obedience, not to mention their esteem and "love," was fundamental to any battlefield undertaking. However, the effort posed complex psychological problems, explaining why as early as the *Art of War*'s "Maneuvering the Army" Sun-tzu noted that "if you impose punishments on the troops before they have become attached, they will not be submissive. If they are not submissive, they will be difficult to employ. If you do not impose punishments after the troops have become attached, they cannot be used."

History has shown that whether they actually mutiny or not, when the commander loses the willing commitment of the troops, they may fail to respond to orders and thereby become useless. Apparently unworried that excessive compassion might result in the commander being unable to risk their lives or even being perceived as weak and effeminate, the classic military writers generally believed that solicitude provided the key. According to "Superior Strategy" in the *Huang-shih Kung*:

The *Military Pronouncements* states: "In his command of the army, the exemplary general governs men as he would want to be treated himself. Spreading his kindness and extending his beneficence, the strength of his officers is daily renewed. In battle they are like the wind arising, their attack is like the release of a pent-up river." Thus our army can be seen but not withstood, can be submitted to but not be conquered. If you lead the men in person, your soldiers will become the most valiant under Heaven.

The *Art of War* initiated this thread of thought in "Configurations of Terrain" by asserting that "when the general regards his troops as young children, they will advance into the deepest valleys with him. When he regards the troops as his beloved children, they will be willing to die with him." However, it further noted the problems that might arise if they are not disciplined as well: "If they are well treated but cannot be employed, if they are loved but cannot be commanded, or when in chaos they cannot be governed, they may be compared to arrogant children and cannot be used." Accordingly, they should be "commanded with the civil and unified through the martial."

Apparently disregarding the negative impact on the commander's awesomeness, most thinkers also agreed that the commander should not live a privileged life but instead share the miseries and difficulties experienced by the troops. According to "Combat Awesomeness" in the *Wei Liao-tzu*: "When the army is toiling on the march, the general must establish himself [as an example]. In the heat he does not set up an umbrella, in the cold he does not wear heavier clothes. On difficult terrain he must dismount and walk. Only after the army's wells are finished does he drink, only after the army's food is cooked does he eat, and only after the army's ramparts are complete does he rest. He must personally experience the same toil and respite. In this fashion even though the army is in the field for a long time, it will neither be old nor exhausted."

Similarly, in his "Superior Strategy," Huang-shih Kung noted that "the *Military Pronouncements* states: 'When the army's wells have not yet been completed, the general does not mention thirst. When the encampment has not yet been secured, the general does not speak about fatigue. When the army's cookstoves have not yet been lit, the general does not speak about hunger. In the winter he doesn't wear a fur robe; in the summer he doesn't use a fan; and in the rain he doesn't set up an umbrella.' This is termed the proper form of behavior for a general."

When combined with solicitude, the impact would be dramatic, just as Huang-shih Kung further noted:

Those who command the army must share tastes and attitudes with the officers and men and confront both safety and danger with them for then the enemy can be attacked. Thus the army will attain full victory and the enemy will be completely destroyed. In antiquity, when outstanding generals commanded armies, there was once a case where the commander was presented with a cask of sweet wine. The general had it poured into the river and shared the drinking of the wine with the officers and men as it flowed downstream. Now a cask of wine is unable to flavor a river of water, but the officers of the Three Armies were all motivated to fight to the death because the flavor and taste reached them personally.

In addition to mentioning the cask of wine in his discussion, Li believed that commanders had to encompass a wide range of virtues and manifest numerous positive attributes. The ancient writers also advocated leading in person. For example, "Combat Awesomeness" states, "Those who engage in combat must take leading in person as their foundation in order to incite the masses and officers, just as the mind controls the four limbs." However, by the T'ang, commanders had long become accustomed to directing the battle from afar, if only because of warfare's vast scope, even though T'ang T'ai-tsung had distinguished himself with his daring and military prowess. Insofar as he has often been viewed as the last general to truly combine civil and martial abilities, to command yet also lead, Wu Ch'i's image still loomed large in T'ang martial circles. Though no doubt exaggerated, his biography in the *Shih Chi* still defined him and what many believed to be the ideal form of a commander's behavior. One particularly well known incident was widely known for centuries:

> Wu Ch'i happened to hear that Marquis Wen of Wei was a Worthy and wanted to serve in his court. Marquis Wen questioned Li K'o about him: "What sort of a man is Wu Ch'i?"
>
> Li K'o replied, "Ch'i is greedy and licentious, but in the employment of troops even the famous general Ssu-ma Jang-chü could not surpass him." Upon hearing this Marquis Wen appointed him as a general. Wu Ch'i attacked Ch'in and seized five cities.
>
> In his position as general, Wu Ch'i's custom was to wear the same clothes and eat the same food as the men in the lowest ranks. When sleeping he did not set out a mat, while on the march he did not ride a horse or in a chariot. He personally packed up his leftover rations and shared all labors and misery with the troops.
>
> Once when one of his soldiers had a blister, he personally sucked out the pus for him. The soldier's mother heard about it and wept. Someone said to her, "Your son is only an ordinary soldier, while the general himself sucked out the pus. What is there to weep about?"
>
> The mother retorted, "That isn't it. In years past Duke Wu sucked his father's blister. His father went to war without hesitating and subsequently died at the hands of the enemy. Now Duke Wu again sucks my son's blister, so I don't know where he will die. For this reason I weep."

However, without the socializing foundation discussed in the chapter's second paragraph (which is itself derived from a similar articulation in the *Hsün-tzu*), Li believed that even exemplary commanders may fail to prove successful.

16

選 士

"SELECTING WARRIORS"

The classics say that if someone unifies the masses of the six armies and commands a field force of a million but lacks a selected (elite) front and instead intermixes [the soldiers] and randomly employs them, the wise will not have any means to unfold their plans, disputers no means to exercise their persuasion, the courageous no means to incite their daring, and the powerful no means to manifest their stalwartness. This would be no different than going forth onto the Central Plains alone, how can victory possibly be seized? Thus Sun-tzu said that "an army without a selected front is termed 'defeated.'"

If you select men by [enticing them with] rewards, rewards will motivate them to advance [into the enemy]; if you employ warriors through [the threat of] punishments, punishments will deter them from retreating. In antiquity those who excelled at selecting men suspended the rewards at the army's middle gate.

Anyone who put forth profound clandestine plans that surpassed the ordinary were awarded the highest rewards in a ritual and titled "officers of wisdom and wise plans."

Those whose words could depart from reason, effectively fly about, and penetrate closed doors could change men's character and snatch their minds were awarded the highest rewards in a ritual and titled "officers with disputative skills."

Those who could gain information about the character and nature of the court members within the enemy's palace were awarded the highest rewards in a ritual and titled "clandestine agents."

Those who knew the mountains, springs, rivers, grasses (pastureland), and halting places and lodges, the road's curves and straightness, were awarded the highest rewards in a ritual and titled "officers with village knowledge."

Those who could fabricate the five weapons and the implements for attack and defense, who were unorthodox, changeable, deceptive, and deceitful, were awarded the highest rewards and treated generously, being termed "officers with [special] skills."

Those who could pull a five picul bow and whose arrows could penetrate several layers of armor, who were skilled in the use of the dagger-ax [*ko*], spear, sword, halberd, who could strike a rhinoceros on land and alligators in the water, who could furtively capture tigers, seize the enemy's flags, and capture their drums, were given the highest rewards, treated generously, and termed "fierce and resolute warriors."

Those who could suddenly jump on horses and hastily race about left and right, who could jump over fortifications and bastions and go in and out of encampments without a trace, were awarded the highest rewards in a ritual, assembled together, and termed "warriors of alacrity."

Those who could race out and back three hundred *li* before nightfall were granted the highest rewards, assembled together, and called "fleet-footed warriors."

Those who had the strength to carry six hundred fifty *chin* fifty paces were granted the highest reward and assembled; those who could carry four hundred twenty *chin* were the next-highest rewards and assembled, all of them being termed "warriors of gigantic strength."

Those who could unfold the five phases, employ the planchette [for divination], speak fluently about the Tao of Heaven, yin and yang, and deception were granted the lowest rewards, assembled, and termed "warriors of skillful techniques."

You should fully exhaust the talents of these ten types of warriors, employing each of them in accord with their Tao. For strategic planning employ "officers of wisdom and wise plans." For discussions employ "officers with disputative skills." To estrange [the enemy's court] and cause them to be separated employ "spies." When entering the territory of the other feudal lords, employ "local guides." For creating and manufacturing the five weapons, employ "warriors of [special] skills." To smash the enemy's sharp front, capture prisoners, defend dangerous places, and attack the strong employ "warriors fierce in the face of the enemy." To stealthily mount sudden strikes and raid and plunder employ "warriors of alacrity." To conduct reconnaissance and report on plans in a timely manner employ "fleet-footed warriors." To destroy the solid and overturn the firm employ "warriors of gigantic strength." To deceive the stupid and strike fear into the dimwitted employ "warriors of skillful techniques."

This is what is referred to as the Tao of entrusting responsibility to the talented, the technique for selecting warriors. After the three kings, from the five hegemons onward those who comprehended this prospered, but those who lost it perished. The Tao for prospering and perishing does not lie in clever wisdom and cultural thoughts but in selecting the capable and having them fully exhaust their efforts.

SAWYER

From Sun-tzu onward the classic military thinkers realized the need for an elite force that might initiate attacks, penetrate the enemy's formations, and cause consternation and chaos. Although the *Art of War* mentions the need for a "properly selected vanguard" in "Configurations of Terrain," in "Planning for the State"

Wu Ch'i was the first to stress psychological issues and background in creating a formidable army, especially elite units:

> Among the people those who have courage and strength should be assembled into one unit. Those who take pleasure in advancing into battle and exerting their strength to manifest their loyalty and courage should be assembled into another unit. Those who can climb high and traverse far, who are nimble and fleet, should be assembled into a unit. Officials of the king who have lost their positions and want to show their merit to their ruler should be assembled into a unit. Those who abandoned their cities or left their defensive positions and want to eradicate the disgrace should also be assembled into a unit.
>
> These five will constitute the army's disciplined, elite troops. With three thousand such men, one can strike out from within and break any encirclement or break into any city from without and slaughter the defenders.

In response to the requirements of warfare's increasing lethality, he equally stressed physical ability in "Evaluating the Enemy":

> Within the army you must have soldiers with the courage of tigers, the strength to easily lift tripods, and the fleetness of barbarian horses. To attack their flags and seize their generals you must have men with such abilities. If you have men such as these, select and segregate them [into special units]; favor and honor them. They are referred to as the "army's fate."
>
> Those who are expert in the use of the five weapons, who are strong and quick, and are intent upon swallowing the enemy, should be given rank and prominence because they can make victory decisive. If you are generous to their parents, wives, and children, encourage them with rewards, and

awe them with punishments, these strong soldiers will solidly hold their positions in formation for a long time. If you can discern and evaluate men such as these, you can attack a force double your strength.

However, Li was not exclusively concerned with creating a stalwart vanguard but instead with selecting the men required for a variety of essential military tasks. In this he followed the extensive categorization preserved in "The King's Wings," a chapter of the *Six Secret Teachings* that distinguishes eighteen major responsibilities and appends appropriate titles. Among the more important are strategists, topographers, and supply personnel, "Officers for Flourishing Awesomeness," and several designated by rubrics such as "Ears and Eyes" and "Officers of Techniques" who are tasked with clandestine or unorthodox functions. (These "Officers of Techniques" were "responsible for spreading slander and falsehood and for calling on ghosts and spirits in order to confuse the mind of the populace." "Roving Officers" were to be entrusted with "spying on the enemy's licentiousness and observing their changes; manipulating their emotions; and observing the enemy's thoughts, acting as spies.")

MINOR JOTTINGS

An annotated translation of "The King's Wings" may be found in my *Seven Military Classics of Ancient China*.

17

勵 士

"INCITING THE WARRIORS"

A classic states that "to stimulate people's minds and incite their *ch'i*; to issue commands and have men take pleasure in hearing them; to flourish the army, mobilize the troops, and have the men take pleasure in combat; and to have the armies clash and blades intersect and cause men to take pleasure in dying lies in combat inciting combat, rewards inciting rewards, and warriors stimulating each other."

Logs and stones have no minds, but when they are endangered, they move, and when settled are tranquil, so how much the more so inspired warriors? In ancient times when the former emperors, kings, and hegemons possessed the realm, they reviewed the army and assessed achievements, assembling the masses at the army's central gate. Those with the greatest accomplishments were awarded gold medallions with purple cords, given embroidered clothes and silk fabrics, and seated on doubly thick woven mats. They were feasted with the [three meats of the] *T'ai-lao* and drank the purest wine. Their fathers and mothers, wives and children were all given light silks and seated on double mats, feasted with [the two meats of the] *Shao-lao*, and drank superior wine.

The commanding general personally bestowed the awards, and the lieutenant generals presented the beakers of wine. The commanding general then proclaimed to the assembly: "Such and such warrior fought so fervently that he forgot himself. His achievements surpassed a million, and thus he is given the highest reward. He beheaded the enemy's leader and seized the commanding general's flag, so his accomplishments are higher than the masses and thus merit the highest rewards. His children, grandchildren, and later posterity will always be distinguished as the family of a *Ch'ing-ta-fu*. His father and mother, wife and children are all being given generous rewards, only their seating and feasting differs in being slightly lower, as you should all know."

Those who ranked next in accomplishments were awarded silver medallions with vermillion ribbons, given embroidered clothes, seated on double mats, feasted with the *Shao-lao*, and drank superior wine. Their fathers and mothers, wives and children were all given light silks, seated on single mats, feasted with chicken and pork, and drank good wine. The lieutenant generals bestowed the rewards, and the brigadiers presented the beakers of wine. The commanding general then proclaimed to the assembly: "The courage of such and such stalwart warrior stands at the head of the Three Armies, his accomplishments have been witnessed in a hundred battles. He beheaded fierce enemy leaders, seized the tiger and panther flags, and his accomplishments surpass all others. He is presented with the next-highest award, and his sons, grandsons, and posterity will always be regarded as a family of great distinction. His father and mother, wife and children are all receiving glorious rewards, with only their feasting and seating being reduced, as you all know."

Those with the least accomplishments were awarded clothes of ordinary silk, seated on single-layer mats, feasted with chickens and pork, and drank good wine. Their fathers and mothers, wives and children stood but were not given rewards or sat but without mats. The brigadiers bestowed the awards, the troops presented the beakers of wine. The commanding general then proclaimed to the assembly: "Such and such stalwart warrior exhausted his strength in the ranks for months and years, so even though he did not snare flags or kill generals, he tread on the battlefield of death. Thus he is presented with the lowest-ranking award, but his sons, grandsons, and posterity will not receive any special designation nor are his father and mother, wife and children seated or feasted, as you should all know."

When the proclamations were finished, those with the highest accomplishments were ordered to rise and bow twice to the commanding general and deferentially say: "Numbering among the king's subordinates, how could we not have preserved the regulations and exhausted out strength? We are ashamed that we have no merit yet enjoy the highest awards." The commanding general then rises from his mat and says: "I am not virtuous yet erroneously was given leadership over the army. I have relied upon your accomplishments. You slew the leaders of the evil and rebellious and displayed their heads, accumulated great merit, and achieved glorious accomplishments. I cannot monopolize the excellence of these achievements." They all withdraw and resume sitting.

Those whose accomplishments rated next are then ordered to bow to those with the highest achievements. Those with the highest achievements then say, "We had no strategy or courage, we merely obeyed the orders of our leaders and thus gained the glory of having advanced into death rather than suffering the disgrace of retreating in order to survive and thus received outstanding rewards. Above they glorify our fathers and mothers, below they extend to our wives and children and will be an inspiration to them."

After they withdraw and are reseated those next [least] in accomplishments are ordered to bow to those with moderate accomplishments. Remaining seated, those with moderate accomplishments say, "We had little courage or resolution but respected the orders of the army's leaders, and victory and deceit were decided in a moment. We have received the next rank of rewards, above they glorify our fathers and mothers, below they extend to our wives and children and will be an inspiration to them." Those who received the lowest awards then withdraw and resume their seats.

When they had stimulated them in this manner, at one conclave inhabitants in towns encouraged those in villages; those in the neighborhoods encouraged those dwelling in the lanes; and fathers persuaded their sons, and wives pressured their husbands. After they had held it twice, the members from the district encouraged those in the province, and friends encouraged each other. After three times, even passersby stimulated each other on the road. When they heard the sound of armaments and armor, they stepped on each other in their haste to go forth. Thereafter no state could withstand even a minor village contingent, and cities lacked sufficiently solid fortifications. So why would there have been any concern that the warriors would not be courageous?!

SAWYER

According to the *Wu-tzu*, Wu Ch'i advised the ruler to "identify men of accomplishment and then honor them with a grand feast while also stimulating those who failed to accomplish anything notable." "Stimulating the Officers," a chapter found in the *Wu-tzu*, sketchily describes an appropriate awards ceremony, one intended to nurture the courage required for combat. Moreover, rather than allowing the commander to haphazardly present the honors, Wu Ch'i clearly intended that they should be granted in a highly structured ritual that featured drinking, feasting, and other actions that would magnify the inherent glory of the moment:

> Marquis Wu had sitting mats set out in the ancestral temple hall, arrayed them into three rows, and held a feast for the officers and chief officials. Those distinguished by their

achievements sat in the front row and were feasted with the finest foods together with three meats served on the most valuable dishes. Those ranked next in accomplishment sat in the middle row and were feasted with fine food served on less lavish vessels. Those who had not accomplished anything noteworthy sat in the last row and were feasted with fine food served on ordinary utensils.

When the feast was over and they came out, he also honored the parents and families of the meritorious outside the temple gate, again according to their accomplishments. He annually sent emissaries to call upon the families of those who had died in the service of the country, bestowing aid on their parents. By so doing he showed that they would not be forgotten.

The specifics of that ceremony, long lost, are unimportant, but the distinctions, however trivial, in vessels, seating, and food no doubt mattered greatly in antiquity. In replicating this event, Li Ch'üan's "Inciting the Warriors" has clearly expanded the detail somewhat. More important, according to material embedded in the *Wu-tzu*, this practice produced superlative results that became visible just three years later when Ch'in mobilized its army and approached the West River commandery. When Wei's officers heard of the incursion, "tens of thousands buckled on their armor and enthusiastically attacked them without waiting for any orders from their superiors." Elated by their victory, Wu Ch'i requested fifty thousand "previously undistinguished men" who, after being augmented by five hundred chariots and three thousand cavalry, went on to destroy a force from Ch'in traditionally said to have numbered five hundred thousand men but no doubt far less, though certainly still vastly superior in numbers and experience.

In early China many of the individual states imposed fairly strict hierarchical organizations on their people, segmenting them into villages, towns, and larger areas for labor mobilization and military obligations. Although the depictions found in the *Chou Li* of the *hsiang-sui* and other systems almost certainly represent idealizations, the fundamental unit was often the hamlet of five families or an artificial but locally based grouping that would be expected to furnish the fighting members of a squad of five. Apart from providing a latent military organization, the continued grouping of men from a single locale ensured a familiarity and camaraderie otherwise unobtainable while simultaneously exploiting innate rivalries that would spur them to greater achievements.

Two centuries later the *Wei Liao-tzu* succinctly isolated several of these motivators:

> In order to stimulate the soldiers, the people's material welfare must be ample. The ranks of nobility, the degree of relationship in death and mourning, the activities by which the people live must be made evident. You must govern the people in accord with their means to life and make distinctions clear in accord with the people's activities. The fruits of the field and their salaries, the feasting of relatives through the rites of eating and drinking, the mutual encouragement in the village ceremonies, mutual assistance in death and the rites of mourning, sending off and greeting the troops — these are what stimulate the people.

Although martial awards ceremonies aided in eliciting courage and ensuring battlefield fervor, they were never considered sufficient in themselves. Ritual could augment the stimulus of rewards, but just as noted in several other chapters (including "Punishments and Rewards," which follows), the specter of punishment was never foregone. Nevertheless, the psychology of courage that evolved during the Warring States period was actually quite complex and sophisticated, never reducible to just the so-called twin handles of punishments and rewards. Perhaps the best summation of the sequential measures that might be systematically employed appears in a section of Sun Pin's *Military Methods*: "When you form the army and assemble the masses, [concentrate upon stimulating their *ch'i*]. When you again decamp and reassemble the army, concentrate upon ordering the soldiers and sharpening their *ch'i*. When you approach the border and draw near the enemy, concentrate upon honing their *ch'i*. When the day for battle has been set, concentrate upon making their *ch'i* decisive. When the day for battle is at hand, concentrate upon expanding their *ch'i*."

Another fragment from the bamboo text of the thematic chapter "Expanding *Ch'i*" speaks about wearing "short coats and coarse clothes to encourage the warriors' determination and hone their *ch'i*," while others from "Killing Officers" add, "Make rewards and emoluments clear. If you treat them deferentially, then the officers will die (for you). If you encourage them with fundamental pleasures, they will die for their native places. [If you importune them with] family relationships, they will die for the ancestral graves. [If you honor them] with feasts, they will die for food and drink. If you have them dwell in tranquility, they will die in the urgency (of defense). If you inquire about their febrile diseases, they will die [for your solicitude]."

A number of displaced strips from the *Military Methods* indicate some of the problems that might be encountered if programs to nurture essential *ch'i* are not successfully implemented among the troops: "If their *ch'i* is not sharp, they will be plodding. When they are plodding, they will not reach (their objective). When they do not reach (their objective), they will lose the advantage. When their *ch'i* is not honed, they will be frightened. When they are frightened, then they will mass together. When their *ch'i* is not decisive, then they will be slack. When they are slack, they will not be focused and will easily disperse. If they easily disperse, they will be defeated when they encounter difficulty." Although feasting can foster fervor and commitment, clearly it was never deemed sufficient in itself.

MINOR JOTTINGS

For an extensive discussion of traditional and contemporary views on courage and its manipulation, see my article "Martial Qi in China: Courage and Spirit in Thought and Military Practice," *Journal of Military and Strategic Studies*, Winter 2008/2009, available at www.jmss.org. China's three early ritual texts — the *Yi Li, Li Chi*, and *Tai Tai Li Chi* — all contain detailed descriptions of various rituals that were performed at the village and higher level, including several with decidedly martial intent such as the archery competition and village feasting ceremony.

18

刑 賞

"PUNISHMENTS AND REWARDS"

The classics state that when Yu Yü Shih distinguished clothes and caps and created distinctive emblems and punishments intended to augment his oversight [of the people], villains did not dare contravene them because the people of the time were simple. T'ang and Wu created the five corporeal punishments, injured the four limbs, and augmented these inflictions by slaying [offenders], yet villainy did not cease because the people were licentious. It wasn't that Yu Yü was not benevolent and T'ang and Wu were brutal, it's just that their Tao differed because of the times.

In olden times those who excelled at governing the realm did not reward benevolence (仁) because if they rewarded benevolence, the people would compete to practice it, and the state would become chaotic. They did not reward wisdom because if they rewarded wisdom, the people would compete to formulate strategies, and the government would become chaotic. They did not reward loyalty because if they rewarded loyalty, the people would compete to be forthright, and rulers would become confused. They did not reward ability because if they rewarded ability, people would compete at cleverness, and affairs would become chaotic. They did not reward courage because if they rewarded courage, men would compete to be at the front, and the army's formations would become chaotic.

Directing the masses with benevolence, employing wisdom in tactical planning, serving the ruler with loyalty, controlling matters through ability, and confronting the enemy courageously — all five are normal for officers. Rewarding these constants will result conflict, and when conflict arises, the administration will be in chaos. When the administration is thrown into chaos, it will not be possible to control [the people] without resorting to punishments. Thus rewards [appear] when loyalty and fidelity have grown thin and are the source of chaos.

Punishments are constraints intended [to ensure] loyalty and fidelity and the source of proscriptions. When punishments are numerous and rewards few, [there will be] no punishments, but when rewards are numerous and punishments few, there will be no rewards. Excessive punishments will not result in goodness, but excessive rewards will result in villainy multiplying. The king prohibits through rewards and stimulates through punishments, he seeks excessiveness rather than goodness, yet the people do good of themselves.

Rewards are civil (*wen*), punishments martial (*wu*). *Wen* and *wu* are the methods of the military and the handles of state. When wise rulers appeared, the manifest things were made to accord with the seasons in order to give comfort to the four quarters. They took hold of the laws and grasped the handles [of punishments and rewards], setting up punishments that accorded with the crime and establishing rewards based upon achievement. By rewarding a single accomplishment, they pleased ten million, by punishing one crime, they frightened ten million. There was no favoritism in granting rewards, no grudges in determining punishment. This behavior might be said to have nurtured the laws of the army and state, the handles of life and slaying.

Thus it is said that the state of someone who is capable of giving life and slaying will certainly be strong, but the state of someone who can nurture life but is incapable of slaying will perish. [However], it is also said that being capable of restoring life to the dead and pardoning killers is best.

The techniques for punishing and rewarding should not be a personal affair but instead always publicly conducted. They were not established just in the times of Yao and Shun nor solely lost in the courts of Chieh [of the Hsi] and Chou [Emperor Hsin of the Shang]. When the Chou acquired these techniques, the realm was governed, but when they lost them, All under Heaven fell into chaos. The Tao for controlling chaos lies in punishments and rewards, not with the rulers of men. Beyond this, despite theories about the universe and the entanglements of the myriad things, the sage does not speak about anything other than life and death.

SAWYER

Despite esteeming Confucian values and Virtue, even Li Ch'üan was compelled by his acceptance of the Taoist viewpoint of devolution to recognize the necessity for rewards and punishments. Accordingly, he discusses them in several chapters, including "Punishments and Rewards," "The Government Executes the Strong," and "Troops." The *T'ai-pai Yin-ching* never offers any information about the differences that may have resulted in rewards and punishments during the process of devolution, but a passage in the *Ssu-ma Fa*'s "Obligations of the Son of Heaven" perhaps provides some background: "The Hsia bestowed rewards in court in order to make the good eminent. The Shang carried out executions in the marketplace to overawe the evil. The Chou granted rewards in court and carried out executions in the marketplace to encourage gentlemen and terrify the common man. Hence the kings of all three dynasties manifested Virtue in the same way."

The incentive value of martial rewards, their ability to stimu-late men to wade into combat and rush into incendiary maelstroms (as noted by Han Fei-tzu), had been well known and consciously exploited long before the classic military theorists analyzed their impact or Sun-tzu advised dividing up the spoils, even bestowing rewards not required by law. Shang oracular inscriptions attest to punishments having been employed for their deterrent value as much as punitive purposes. Nevertheless, formulating mea-sures that would effectively implement the "twin handles" posed an extremely thorny problem that entailed perplexing emotional and behavioral implications.

Punishments and rewards were invariably employed in com-bination, a practice that increased the administrative complexity as authorities sought the right balance. Shang Yang, for example, emphasized punishment and advocated few rewards, with the latter being given only for military accomplishment and agricul-tural achievement. Shang Yang's partisans (rather simplistically) believed that severely punishing minor infractions would pre-vent major offenses from occurring, a view visible in Li's state-ment that "when punishments are numerous and rewards few, [there will be] no punishments, but when rewards are numerous and punishments few, there will be no rewards." Conversely, the Confucians felt that inner emotional factors (such as a sense of shame) were more important. Nevertheless, in the military realm the debate was generally resolved by opting for strict organiza-tion, draconian punishments, and mutual responsibility much as the regulations preserved in the latter half of the *Wei Liao-tzu* indicate.

The pre-T'ang military writings outlined the factors and con-straints that had to be observed if rewards and punishments were to be credible. These included adherence to standards rather than arbitrariness, universal applicability and inescapability, and timeliness. Thus, Huang-shih Kung stated that "rewards and punishments must be as certain as Heaven and Earth for then the general can employ the men." In the *Wei Liao-tzu*'s "Military Instructions, II" the T'ai Kung is quoted as purportedly having said that "rewards should be like mountains, punishments like valleys." A *Six Secret Teachings* passage with obvious echoes in Li's disquisition provides further elaboration:

> King Wen asked the T'ai Kung: "Rewards are the means to preserve the encouragement [of the good], punishments the means to display the rectification of evil. By rewarding one man, I want to stimulate a hundred, by punishing one man rectify the multitude. How can I do it?"
>
> The T'ai Kung replied: "In general, credibility is valued when employing rewards and certainty when employing punishments. When rewards are trusted and punishments inevitable wherever the eye sees and the ear hears, then even where they do not see or hear there is no one who will not be transformed in their secrecy."

In a passage previously cited from "Martial Plans," the *Wei Liao-tzu* advised that universal application was crucial to ensuring the commander's awesomeness: "In general, executions provide the means to illuminate the martial. If by executing one man the entire army will quake, kill him. If by rewarding one man ten thousand men will rejoice, reward him. In executing, value the great; in rewarding, value the small. If someone should be killed, then even though he is honored and powerful, he must be executed because this will be punishment that reaches the pinnacle. When rewards extend down to the cowherds and stable boys, rewards flow down [to the lowest]." The *Huang-shih Kung* added the observation that "the *Military Pronouncements* states: 'The army employs rewards as its external form and punishments as its internal substance.' When rewards and punishments are clear, the general's awesomeness is effected."

As Li notes in his discussion, punishments and rewards were often conceived of in terms of the martial (*wu* 武) and civil (*wen* 文). In discussing the general issue of punishment and command, in "Maneuvering the Army" the *Art of War* states that "if you command them with the civil and unify them through the martial, this is what is referred to as 'being certain to take them.'" The greater question then was how *wen* and *wu* might be weighted, how order might be imposed and difficulties resolved within the army without the fundamentally complementary realms becoming severely imbalanced. Extreme situations such as major defeats posed fundamentally intractable problems because martial law required virtually decimating the troops, clearly an unacceptable option in view of the ongoing need for manpower, no doubt accounting for the *Ssu-ma Fa*'s advice not to punish anyone in cases of great defeat.

On the other hand, contravening expected practice entailed different problems and might foster disdain for the regulations and their associated punishments. The effectiveness of rewards and punishments was deemed so important that one of Sun-tzu's fundamental criteria for evaluating potential enemies was "whose rewards and punishments are clearer?" However, frequent employment of either was considered a sign of disorder; therefore, in "Maneuvering the Army," the *Art of War* notes that frequent rewards indicate distress in the army, frequent punishments indicate difficulty.

19

地 勢

"CONFIGURATIONS
OF TERRAIN"

The classics state that those who excelled at warfare exploited the terrain's constraints and gained victory through strategic power just the way the terrain's strategic configuration causes round stones to roll down a thousand-fathom mountain slope.

A thousand-fathom [drop] is certainly precipitous terrain while round stones embody the power of turning. But if the terrain does not drop off a thousand fathoms and the round stones are placed in a depression, they will no longer revolve. If the mountainside drops a thousand fathoms but the stones are not round, tossing flat and rectangular rocks will just result in a pile, they will not be able to move any further. When the land is not precipitous, it cannot cause even round stones to roll, so stones that are not round cannot go down into the deepest valley or ravine. Thus it is said that armies become strong by taking advantage of the terrain and that the terrain is solidified by the army.

Those who excelled at employing the military did not approach high mountain ridges nor contravene hillocks behind them. They turned their backs to yin and embraced yang, nurtured life, and dwelled in the substantial for then the army did not suffer the hundred illnesses. For this reason when the feudal lords fought in their own territory, it was termed "dispersive terrain." When they entered the borders of others but not very deeply, it was called "light terrain." When the terrain was advantageous to both the enemy and themselves, it was called "contentious terrain." When both forces could go forth, it was called "traversable terrain." When the area was subordinate to three feudal states, it was called "focal terrain." Deeply penetrating the enemy's territory where cities lie was called "heavy terrain." Areas where there were mountainous forests, wetlands, marshes, ravines, and defiles were called "endangering terrain." When advancing and withdrawing along tortuous paths and narrows, where a few of the enemy could strike the army's masses, was called "encircled terrain." Where urgent warfare would lead to preservation but shunning combat result in perishing, it was called "fatal terrain."

Therefore, on dispersive terrain one should not engage in warfare, on light terrain not tarry, on contentious terrain not attack, and on traversable terrain not become cut off. On focal terrain unite with your allies, and on heavy terrain you must plunder [for provisions]. You must quickly move through dangerous terrain, resort to strategy on encircled terrain, and engage in combat on fatal terrain.

For this reason there are fortified towns that are not attacked because it would not cohere with the strategy. There is terrain for which one does not contend because no advantage is visible. There are orders from the ruler that are not obeyed because they will not facilitate military affairs.

The strategic power of terrain empowers the Three Armies. Superlative generals exploit the terrain's constraints, wise generals respect them, but ordinary generals ignore them yet hope to fortuitously achieve complete victory just as if turtles could fly or snakes could dance. It has never happened.

SAWYER

One of the distinctive features of traditional Chinese military science has always been an emphasis upon recognizing variations in the terrain and then exploiting topographical features through appropriate tactics. Even though effective commanders had been cognizant of these issues long before the *Art of War*'s compilation, the recognition that topography is fundamental to military tactics, the systematic classification of terrain types, and the correlation of basic operational principles all received their first formulation in several chapters of the *Art of War*, and their inception is therefore generally attributed to Sun-tzu, who propounded the fundamental principle:

> Configuration of terrain is an aid to the army. Analyzing the enemy, taking control of victory, estimating ravines and defiles, the distant and near, is the Tao of the superior general. One who knows these and employs them in combat will certainly be victorious. One who does not know these nor employ them in combat will certainly be defeated.

Reflecting his thinking in "Earth Has No Dangerous Ravines or Impediments," Li commences by pointing out the limitations of the strategic power analogy. However, unlike men stones are inflexible, nonsentient objects incapable of self-initiated action, and it is clear from the remainder of the chapter and other pronouncements in the *T'ai-pai Yin-ching* that he did not intend to absolutely deny the strategic effects of topographical features, merely shift the interpretation to focus on the effects of human exploitation. Thus he asserts that "armies become strong by taking advantage of the terrain, and the terrain is solidified by the army" and "superlative generals exploit the terrain's constraints."

Nine terrains are frequently associated with Sun-tzu because that is the title of his famous chapter 11: dispersive, light, contentious, traversable, focal, heavy, entrapping, encircled, and fatal. However, in "Configurations of Terrain," the *Art of War* separately states that "the major configurations of terrain are accessible, suspended, stalemated, constricted, precipitous, and expansive." The book actually identifies more than twenty distinct configurations and describes several additional deadly land formations, such as "Heaven's Well," in three focal chapters, "Nine Changes," "Configurations of Terrain," and of course "Nine Terrains" itself. The terms overlap to some extent, and the definitions and associated tactics vary somewhat, but they are never contradictory.

Having commented extensively on all three chapters, Li Ch'üan was thoroughly familiar with the *Art of War*'s categories, definitions, and associated operational tactics, but he opted to adopt those delineated in "Nine Terrains." According to the original text:

> When the feudal lords fight in their own territory, it is "dispersive terrain." When they enter someone else's territory, but not deeply, it is "light terrain." If when we occupy it, it will be advantageous to us while if they occupy it, it will be advantageous to them, it is "contentious terrain." When we can go and they can also come, it is "traversable terrain." Land of the feudal lords surrounded on three sides such that whoever arrives first will gain the masses of All under Heaven is "focal terrain." When one penetrates deeply into enemy territory, bypassing numerous cities, it is "heavy terrain." Where there are mountains and forests, ravines and defiles, wetlands and marshes, wherever the road is difficult to negotiate, it is "entrapping terrain." Where the entrance is constricted, the return is circuitous, and with a small number they can strike our masses, it is "encircled terrain." Where if one fights with intensity he will survive but if he does not fight with intensity he will perish, it is "fatal terrain."

No doubt in consequence he also adopted the chapter's operational recommendations:

On dispersive terrain do not engage the enemy. On light terrain do not stop. On contentious terrain do not attack. On traversable terrain do not allow your forces to become isolated. On focal terrain unite and form alliances [with nearby feudal lords.] On heavy terrain plunder for provisions. On entrapping terrain move [through quickly]. On encircled terrain use strategy. On fatal terrain engage in battle.

Apart from these named configurations, Sun-tzu also mentioned problematic obstacles such as rivers, wetlands, mountains, marshes, and salt flats and offered some tactical principles that Li Ch'üan quotes at the start of the third paragraph and recur in other chapters, including: "Now, the army likes heights and abhors low areas, esteems the sunny (yang) and disdains the shady (yin). It nourishes life and occupies the substantial. An army that avoids the hundred illnesses is said to be certain of victory. Where there are hills and embankments, you must occupy the yang side, keeping them to the right rear."
Throughout his "Configurations of Terrain," Li thus basically synthesizes Sun-tzu's pronouncements, thereby creating a coherent doctrine presumably applicable in his own era. He even condenses and rephrases the famous dictum that "there are roads that are not followed; there are armies that are not attacked; there are fortified cities that are not assaulted; there is terrain for which one does not contend; and there are commands from the ruler that are not accepted."
Finally, although the *T'ai-pai Yin-ching* never provides an elucidation, the category of fatal terrain deserves notice. In the *Art of War*, it is characterized as a place "where if one fights with intensity, he will survive, but if he does not fight with intensity, he will perish," or, in other words, a desperate battle situation. Rather than choosing them, armies normally find themselves unexpectedly thrust into hopeless situations. However, in his commentary to the *Art of War*, Li notes that Han Hsin astutely arrayed his troops against a river so that they would be compressed and have no alternative to fighting fervently against a superior foe. In order to elicit the surpassing effort needed to be victorious, he

thereby risked defeat and the possibility that his men might just collapse and be slaughtered. However, in addition to asserting that "on fatal terrain you must do battle" and "on fatal terrain I show them that we will not live," the *Art of War* observes that "it is the nature of the army to defend when encircled; to fight fervently when unavoidable; and to follow orders when compelled [by circumstances]."

MINOR JOTTINGS:

The famous *Art of War* analogy for strategic power is conceived in terms of logs and stones: "One who employs strategic power commands men in battle as if he were rolling logs and stones. The nature of wood and stone is to be quiet when stable but to move when on precipitous ground. If they are square they stop, if round they tend to move. Thus the strategic power of one who excels at employing men in warfare is comparable to rolling round boulders down a thousand-fathom mountain. Such is the strategic configuration of power."

20

兵 形

"MILITARY DISPOSITION"

The classics state that when armies are mobilized, they have both form and spirit. Flags and pennants, gongs and armor are manifestations of form; wisdom, strategy, plans, and military affairs are manifestations of spirit. Thus victory in combat and seizing through attacks are matters of form, but they are employed through spirit. Vacuity and substance, change and transformation are accomplishments of spirit that are employed through form. Form is rough but spirit refined. When there is nothing that has form, nothing can be observed, when spirit has no content, it cannot be investigated. Form can appear deranged and affairs externally befuddled, yet spirit remains secretive and fully encompasses affairs within. Observing external form, spirit is not discernible; observing spirit, affairs are not seen. For this reason comparisons must be employed.

For example, dragging faggots to raise dust creates the impression of massive forces, reducing the number of fires for cooking and extinguishing torches gives the appearance of fewness. Being courageous but not resilient, courageously deploying opposite the enemy but then quickly fleeing gives the appearance of retreating. Setting observation posts throughout constricted mountainous and marshy terrain gives the appearance of advancing; interspersing glistening armor among the trees gives the appearance of strength; furled flags lying about, silent drums, and the solitude of desertion give the appearance of weakness.

Thus it is said the army's appearance can be likened to a potter shaping clay or a metal smith casting metal as they make them square or round or into bells or cauldrons. Neither metal nor clay have constant form, they acquire their names through work. Thus deployments do not have any fixed configuration of power, they are shaped in accord with the enemy. Therefore, at the extreme the army approaches being formless for then spies cannot discern its nature, and wise strategists cannot make plans against it. [Sun-tzu said], "In accord with the enemy's disposition, I impose measures upon the masses that produce victory, but the masses are unable to fathom them. Men all know the disposition through which I achieved victory, but no one knows the configuration through which I controlled the victory." Unless form relies upon spirit, it cannot be changed and transformed; unless spirit responds to the enemy, it cannot formulate wise strategies. Thus water controls its configuration in accord with the terrain, armies fashion victory in response to the enemy.

SAWYER

In earlier chapters Li Ch'üan expressed the fundamental idea that plans and intentions must be concealed, that deception should be employed to confuse and manipulate the enemy — two significantly different objectives. By describing a number of commonly recurring battlefield phenomena and correlating them with their underlying reality, the *Art of War* initiated the art of observationally based intelligence in a famous paragraph found in "Maneuvering the Army":

If [an enemy] in close proximity remains quiet, they are relying on their tactical occupation of ravines. If while far off they challenge you to battle, they want you to advance [because] they occupy easy terrain to their advantage.

If large numbers of trees move, they are approaching. If there are many [visible] obstacles in the heavy grass, it is to make us suspicious. If the birds take flight, there is an ambush. If the animals are afraid, [enemy] forces are mounting a sudden attack.

If dust rises high up in a sharply defined column, chariots are coming. If it is low and broad, the infantry is advancing. If it is dispersed in thin shafts, they are gathering firewood. If it is sparse, coming and going, they are encamping.

One who speaks deferentially but increases his preparations will advance. One who speaks belligerently and advances hastily will retreat.

One whose light chariots first fan out to the sides is deploying [for battle].

One who seeks peace without setting any prior conditions is [executing] a stratagem.

One whose troops race off but [who] deploys his army into formation is implementing a predetermined schedule.

One [whose troops] half advance and half retreat is enticing you.

Those who stand about leaning on their weapons are hungry. If those who draw water drink first, they are thirsty. When they see potential gain but do not know whether to advance, they are tired.

Where birds congregate it is empty. If the enemy cries out at night, they are afraid. If the army is turbulent, the general lacks severity. If their flags and pennants move about, they are in chaos. If the officers are angry, they are exhausted.

If they kill their horses and eat the meat, the army lacks grain. If they hang up their cooking utensils and do not return to camp, they are exhausted invaders.

One whose troops repeatedly congregate in small groups here and there, whispering together, has lost the masses. One who frequently grants rewards is in deep distress. One who frequently imposes punishments is in great difficulty. One who is at first excessively brutal and then fears the masses is the pinnacle of stupidity.

One who has emissaries come forth with offerings wants to rest for a while.

If their troops are aroused and approach our forces, only to maintain their positions without engaging in battle or breaking off the confrontation, you must carefully investigate it.

Military analysts quickly compiled a virtual catalog of observations. Once these phenomenal correlations became widely known, astute commanders began to fabricate them in order to deceive and thereby manipulate observers who remained dependent upon simple sensory means, both visual and auditory. Among the earliest deceptions were dragging brush to magnify the army's size or give the impression of approaching forces; feigned retreats; setting out flags and pennants; and deliberately concealing reality by masking appearance and operating silently, conveying a pervasive sense of desolation and abandonment. More active measures also evolved, such as feinting east and striking west, moving troops under concealment of darkness or forests or deliberately seeming to withdraw them but reinforcing the army at night or changing flags and emblems to cause the misidentification of units and commanders. (All these manifestations well cohere with the idea of "determining the form of others but being without form yourself" [形人而我無形] found in the *Art of War*'s "Vacuity and Substance.")

In response, theoreticians warned about the possibility of deception and advised operational measures. For example, to preclude being lured into an ambush by a feigned retreat, in "Obligations of the Son of Heaven," the *Ssu-ma Fa* advised: "In antiquity they did not pursue a fleeing enemy too far nor follow a retreating army too closely. By not pursuing them too far, it was difficult to draw them into a trap; by not pursuing so closely as to catch up, it was hard to ambush them." Later writers would emphasize the need to determine whether they were actually panicked and therefore disordered or were cloaking order with apparent chaos.

In his *Art of War* commentary to "Initial Estimations," Li notes that the army never wearies of employing deception and cites four examples of successfully fabricating a deceptive appearance. In the first Liu Pang was tricked by the Hsiung-nu, who feigned weakness by sending all their stalwart warriors out of the camp, thereby enticing the new emperor into attacking after mistakenly concluding he could easily vanquish a paltry enemy. The other three examples include Sun Pin's reduction of the army's fires to deceive P'ang Chüan into thinking his forces had been deserting, prompting him to race forward with only light troops into the darkness of Ma-ling's confined valley, where he was exterminated; Han Hsin's causing a flurry of activity downstream when he intended to cross upstream; and an incident in which flags were deliberately arrayed to mislead an enemy commander, which is now preserved in the *Tso Chuan*:

> During the Spring and Autumn period, when the lord of Chin was advancing to attack the state of Ch'i, the lord of Ch'i ascended a mountain to observe Chin's army. Chin's forces had established outposts throughout the strategic mountain and marshy areas and had invariably set out flags even where the army would not venture, indicating an expansive deployment. Moreover, they had real men drive their chariots but dummies man the right side of each vehicle. Behind the flags flying on each chariot, they affixed brushwood that dragged in the dust. When the lord of Ch'i saw this, he feared their large numbers and quickly fled.

Historically attempted infrequently — and even less often successfully, though occasionally with dramatic success — deception was thus considered crucial to military activities. However, as already discussed, deception was not the only means for preventing the enemy from penetrating plans and discerning intention. Instead, imposing absolute secrecy and maintaining an unfathomable demeanor, becoming formless and unknowable, was considered the pinnacle. Although already articulated in the *Art of War*, Li adopted a relatively new approach by framing the discussion in terms of form and spirit, the latter of course poignant with connotations of sagely wisdom. Intrinsically interrelated is the idea of plasticity, that the army is not confined to any particular form, and is thus inherently formless in the sense of not having any predetermined deployment or requisite tactics.

Sun-tzu initiated this thrust by pointing out that the army has to be responsive rather than inflexibly configured in either form or intent:

> The army's disposition of force is like water. Water's configuration avoids heights and races downward. The army's disposition of force avoids the substantial and strikes the vacuous. Water configures its flow in accord with the terrain; the army controls its victory in accord with the enemy. Thus the army does not maintain any constant strategic configuration of power, water has no constant shape. One who is able to change and transform in accord with the enemy and wrest victory is termed spiritual.

In accord with the idea that "when you mobilize the army and form strategic plans, you must be unfathomable," the classic military writers from Sun-tzu onward emphasized formless because of the twofold benefits. First, preventing the enemy from anticipating and then undertaking nullifying action; and second, creating doubt, thereby forcing them (as Sun-tzu advocated) to defend against all possibilities, as these slightly rearranged and abridged passages from the *Art of War* indicate:

> The location where we will engage the enemy must not become known to them. If it is not known, then the positions

146

they must prepare to defend will be numerous. If the positions the enemy prepares to defend are numerous, then the forces we will engage will be few.

If we can determine the enemy's disposition of forces while we have no perceptible form, we can concentrate our forces while the enemy is fragmented. If we are concentrated into a single force while they are fragmented into ten, then we attack them with ten times their strength. Thus we are many and the enemy few. If we can attack their few with our many, those whom we engage in battle will be severely constrained.

Thus when someone excels in attacking, the enemy does not know where to mount his defense; when someone excels at defense, the enemy does not know where to attack. Subtle! Subtle! It approaches the formless. Spiritual! Spiritual! It attains the soundless. Thus he can be the enemy's Master of Fate.

Therefore, as Li Ch'üan also notes, "The pinnacle of military deployment approaches the formless." Accordingly, in Sun-tzu's conception, even the army's officers and troops should be kept ignorant of an operation's chosen tactics, resulting in people being mystified but secrecy and future possibilities also being preserved: "In accord with the enemy's disposition, we impose measures on the masses that produce victory, but the masses are unable to fathom them. Men all know the disposition by which we attain victory, but no one knows the configuration through which we control the victory. Thus a victorious battle [strategy] is not repeated, the configurations of response are inexhaustible."

Finally, the idea of responsiveness, of being sensitive to the nature of the enemy's forces, tactics, and command qualifications and responding accordingly (though certainly not mechanistically) appears in the last paragraph. In his commentary to the *Art of War*'s statement that "armies fashion victory in accord with the enemy," Li observes: "If you do not base [your tactics] on the enemy's strategic power, how can you control it? Light troops cannot endure for long, so if they mount a defense, they will certainly be defeated. Heavy troops, if you provoke them, will come forth. Angry troops can be insulted, strong armies can be enervated. If the commanding general is arrogant, be deferential, if he is greedy, then profit him, if he is suspicious, employ estrangement agents. Thus one controls the victory in accord with the enemy."

MINOR JOTTINGS:

Rather than the consequences of victory (which were substantial), Han Hsin's ploy was made even more memorable by his imaginative use of large earthenware jars lashed together with ropes to ferry his men across the turbulent river, a measure necessitated by having employed all his boats to accomplish the ruse.

Water was frequently employed in preimperial military discussions and analogies (as well as a focal subject in contemplative Taoist books including the *Tao Te Ching* and *Huai-nan Tzu*) because of its unique properties including incompressibility, flow characteristics, power, and unrelenting impact.

The numerous deceitful and deceptive measures that evolved over the course of Chinese history are discussed in my *Tao of Spycraft: Intelligence Theory and Practice in Traditional China* and my *Tao of Deception: Unorthodox Warfare in Historic and Modern China*.

21

作 戰

"WAGING WAR"

The classics state that in antiquity those who excelled in directing men in combat might be compared to rolling logs and stones. It is the nature of logs and stones to move when round and be still when square. They move not because they have the ability to move but because the strategic configuration of power makes it unavoidable. Stillness does not result from any capacity to stop but because the strategic configuration of power makes it impossible not to stop.

When engaging in combat, if men fight on their own terrain, they will be inclined to scatter, but if you cast them onto fatal terrain, they will fight. Those who scatter do so not because they are able to but because the strategic situation compels it; those who fight do so not because they are able to but because the strategic situation compels it.

Moving and stopping do not lie with logs and stones but are controlled by men; scattering and fighting do not lie with men but are controlled by the strategic configuration of power. For this reason you should engage in combat with men in accord with the strategic configuration of power.

Engaging in combat before seeing the advantages of the situation will certainly result in even massive armies being defeated. However, if advantages can be perceived, even though the numbers might be few, victory in combat is certain. "Advantage" means a shortcoming for them and strength for us. Arise when you perceive advantage, desist when there are no advantages. [Commanders] who can perceive advantage and exploit opportunities are material for emperors and kings. Thus it is said that "when the moment [for action] arrives, there isn't time to take a breath." Preceding [the moment] is excessive but acting afterward too late.

When advantage can be perceived, it must not be lost, when you meet the moment, you cannot be doubtful. If you fail to exploit advantages and transgress the moment, you will instead suffer misfortune. When there's a thunderclap, there isn't time to cover your ears, when there's a flash of lightening not enough time to close your eyes. Advance as if startled, employ [the army] as if deranged — this is the way to control men in battle through advantage.

When engaging in combat, keep rivers and marshes on the left, mounds and hills on the right, heights to the rear, and declinations to the front. Occupy life-sustaining terrain and strike those on deadly ground. This is the way to direct men fighting on level terrain.

When pressing an enemy, do not force them too close to rivers because they will know death is inescapable and strongly resist. Since animals under duress still have fighting spirit and ants and scorpions have poison, how much the more so men? Allow half of them to cross over before suddenly striking because those in the front will have escaped [the water] while those in the midst of crossing will envy them and lack a mind to fight. If the enemy is moving upstream, intercept them in the river. This is the method for directing men in riverine combat.

If there are mountain ranges, ravines and valleys, or narrows and constrictions to the left and right and you encounter the enemy in them, you should conceal your gongs and drums in the mountains, hide your flags and pennants in the forest, ascend the heights and send your reconnaissance out far, and then go forth where there are no men or horses. This is the way to direct men in valley warfare.

The advantages of strategic power facilitate military activities. Mountains, rivers, and plains are all places for warfare. Those who excel in employing the army realize victory through according with the facilitation [provided by strategic power], gain strength through terrain, and seize [others] through strategic plans. This is the way to have men engage in combat through strategic power. Thus [they gain victory] just like water poured out from a pitcher swooshes down a roof top without congealing or bamboo [seems] to meet the knife and come apart by itself, without any further exertion, after several sections have been split.

SAWYER

This chapter not only revisits the crucial concept of strategic power previously encountered in "Configurations of Terrain," particularly the idea that "one who employs strategic power commands men in battle as if he were rolling logs and stones," but also provides the clearest analysis found in the *T'ai-pai Yin-ching*. Thereafter Li raises the intertwined questions of advantage and timeliness, the latter for the first time in the book, before commenting on a number of terrain issues derived from the *Art of War*. ("Waging War" not only quotes or paraphrases extensively from Sun-tzu's work, even the chapter's very title comes from the *Art of War*. However, the contents are entirely different because Sun-tzu's disquisition focuses on the adverse consequences of prolonged warfare.)

Although historical events clearly show timeliness to always be a crucial factor in warfare, it is not a particularly focal subject in the classic military writings. Thus it is not surprising that Li drew extensively upon the only passage that pondered the subject, one found in "The Army's Strategic Power" in the *Six Secret Teachings*:

One who excels at warfare will await events in the situation without making any movement. When he sees he can be victorious, he will arise; if he sees he cannot be victorious, he will desist. Thus it is said he does not have any fear, he does not vacillate. Of the many harms that can beset an army, vacillation is the greatest. Of disasters that can befall an army, none surpasses doubt.

One who excels in warfare will not lose an advantage when he perceives it nor be doubtful when he meets the moment. One who loses an advantage or lags behind the time for action will, on the contrary, suffer from disaster. Thus the wise follow the time and do not lose an advantage, the skillful are decisive and have no doubts. For this reason when there is a sudden clap of thunder, there isn't time to cover the ears; when there's a flash of lightning, there isn't time to close the eyes. Advance as if suddenly startled, employ your troops as if deranged. Those who oppose you will be destroyed, those who come near will perish. Who can defend against such an attack?

Another chapter in the *Six Secret Teachings*, "Preserving the State's Territory," even more emphatically urges action rather than passivity:

When the sun is at midday, you should dry things. If you grasp a knife, you must cut. If you hold an ax, you must attack.

If, at the height of day, you do not dry things in the sun, this is termed losing the time. If you grasp a knife but do not cut anything, you will lose the moment for profits. If you hold an ax but do not attack, bandits will come.

If trickling streams are not blocked, they will become great rivers. If you don't extinguish the smallest flames, what will you do about a great conflagration? If you don't eliminate the two-leaf sapling, how will you use your ax [when the tree has grown]?

The martial thinkers tended to focus on determining the appropriate or incipient moment (*chi* 機), the right time as sanctioned or indicated by Heaven (*t'ien shih* 天 時), a concept already encountered in earlier chapters. However, background echoes include several verses found in the *Tao Te Ching*'s "Act Actionlessly":

> Plan against the difficult while it remains easy,
> Act upon the great while it is still minute.
> The realm's difficult affairs invariably commence with the easy;
> The realm's great affairs inevitably arise from the minute.
> For this reason the Sage never acts against the great,
> So he can achieve greatness.

Part of the chapter ponders the challenges as well as the opportunities posed by fighting alongside rivers. Although numerous problems can arise, after mentioning the general rules for deployment (which originate in the *Art of War*), Li rationalizes waiting for half the men to cross before launching an attack in terms of the soldiers' psychology. According to the original *Art of War* passage embedded in "Maneuvering the Army":

> After crossing rivers you must distance yourself from them. If the enemy is fording a river to advance, do not confront them in the water. When half their forces have crossed, it will be advantageous to strike them. If you want to engage the enemy in battle, do not array your forces near the river to confront the invader but look for tenable ground and occupy the heights. Do not confront the current's flow. This is the way to deploy the army where there are rivers.

Despite Fu Chien's debacle in the Wei-Chin period, it was well known that riverside deployments can be turned to great advantage. However, two situations must be avoided: being pressed against the water by a force on the interior side (despite Han Hsin's adroit exploitation of just these circumstances, as already mentioned) and compressing the enemy onto fatal terrain by encircling an enemy alongside a river, the mirror situation. The psychology of all these circumstances—fatal terrain, being caught in the midst of a river, and being besieged in a city—is essentially the same: leaving an opening will subvert the will to fight and entice the men to flee, resulting in seizing the objective or defeating the enemy with minimal cost.

Finally, Li's advice for mountain warfare turns Sun-tzu's warning around: "When the army encounters ravines and defiles, wetlands with reeds and tall grass, mountain forests or areas with heavy, entangled undergrowth on the flanks, you must thoroughly search them because they are places where an ambush or spies would be concealed." Numerous tactics for extricating an army from disadvantageous circumstances in the mountains, valleys, and similar difficult terrain would quickly develop in the Warring States period and may be found in the *Wu-tzu* and the later chapters of the *Six Secret Teachings*. For example, "Responding to Change" in the former includes two tactical solutions to the problems encountered in valley warfare:

> Marquis Wu asked: "If I encounter the enemy in a deep valley, where gorges and defiles abound to the sides, while his troops are numerous and ours few, what should I do?"
>
> Wu Ch'i replied: "Traverse hilly regions, forests, valleys, deep mountains, and vast wetlands quickly, departing from them posthaste. Do not be dilatory. If in high mountains or a deep valley the armies should suddenly encounter each other, you should first beat the drums and set up a clamor, taking advantage of it to advance your archers and crossbowmen, both shooting the enemy and taking prisoners. Carefully investigate their degree of control: if they are confused, then attack without doubt."
>
> Marquis Wu asked: "On the left and right are high mountains, while the land is extremely narrow and confined. If

when we meet the enemy we dare not attack them yet cannot escape, what should we do?"

Wu Ch'i replied: "This is referred to as valley warfare. Even if your troops are numerous, they are useless. Summon your talented officers to confront the enemy, the nimble footed and sharpest weapons to be at the forefront. Divide your chariots and array your cavalry, concealing them on all four sides several *li* apart, so that they will not show their weapons. The enemy will certainly assume a solid defensive formation, not daring to either advance or retreat. Thereupon display your flags and array your banners, withdraw outside the mountains, and encamp. The enemy will invariably be frightened, and your chariots and cavalry should then harass them, not permitting them any rest. This is the Tao for valley warfare."

The comprehensive *Six Secret Teachings* actually devotes a dedicated chapter, "Divided Valleys," to this exact situation. One example should suffice to illustrate the tactical approach:

King Wu queried the T'ai Kung: "Suppose we have led the army deep into the territory of the feudal lords, where we encounter the enemy in the midst of a steep valley. I have mountains on our left, water on the right. The enemy has mountains on the right, water on the left. They divide the valley with us in a standoff. If we choose to defend our position, I want to be solid and victorious if we want to fight. How should we proceed?"

The T'ai Kung replied: "If you occupy the left side of a mountain, you must urgently prepare [against an attack from the] right side. If you occupy the right side of a mountain, you should urgently prepare [against an attack from] the left. If the valley has a large river but you don't have boats and oars, you should use the Heavenly Huang to cross the Three Armies over. Those that have crossed should widen the road considerably in order to improve your fighting position. Use the Martial Assault chariots at the front and rear; deploy your strong crossbowmen into ranks; and solidify all your lines and formations. Employ the Martial Assault chariots to block off all the intersecting roads and entrances to the valley. Set your flags out on high ground. This posture is referred to as an Army Citadel.

In general, the method for valley warfare is for the Martial Assault chariots to be in the forefront and the Large Covered chariots to act as a protective force. Your skilled soldiers and strong crossbowmen should cover the left and right flanks. Three thousand men will comprise a contingent that must be deployed in an assault formation. Improve the positions the soldiers occupy. Then the Army of the Left should advance to the left, the Army of the Right to the right, and the Army of the Center to the front, all attacking and advancing together. Those that have already fought should return to their detachment's original positions, the units fighting and resting in succession until you have won."

MINOR JOTTINGS:

The influence of the *Huai-nan Tzu* can be seen in Li's statement that "preceding [the moment] is excessive but acting afterward too late" because an identical statement (and similar concepts) appear in its "Yüan Tao."

The original *Art of War* passage advising tactics for riverine warfare states, "Do not confront the current's flow" because fighting against the current is inherently disadvantageous. Sun Pin accordingly predicted defeat for armies (navies) that contravened the current's flow. However, Li substitutes "if the enemy is moving upstream, intercept them in the river."

22

攻 守

"ATTACK AND DEFENSE"

The classics state that land is the means to nurture the common people, cities the means to defend terrain, and warfare the means to defend cities. Within, by gaining the love of the people, they can mount a defense; without, deriving awesomeness from them, they can engage in warfare. Thereafter, one whose strength is insufficient should assume the defensive, one who has surpassing strength should attack.

The method for attacking an enemy is to first sever their support and ensure that they cannot be rescued from outside. Estimate the amount of grain within the city and calculate their daily consumption. If their provisions are plentiful but their inhabitants few, assault but do not besiege them; if their provisions are few but people numerous, besiege but do not assault them.

When their strength has not yet been enervated, their grain not yet exhausted, and their fortifications still solid but the city is taken, it represents the very pinnacle of assault techniques. If their strength has been compromised, their grain exhausted, and their fortifications ruined but it cannot be seized, it represents the pinnacle of strength.

Now the method for mounting city defenses is to have all the stalwart men within the city compose one contingent, the robust women another, and the old and weak among the men and women a third. Do not let the three contingents meet each other. If the stalwart men encounter the robust women, they will waste their strength and licentious activities will result. If the robust women encounter the old and weak, the old will cause them to feel grief while the weak will cause them to be consumed by pity. When grief and pity fill their minds, it will cause [even] courageous men to ponder [their plight] and the stalwart not to fight.

Accordingly [the *Art of War*] asserts that "when men excel in assaults, the enemy does not know where to mount a defense; when men excel at defense, the enemy does not know where to attack. Subtle, subtle, it approaches the formless; spiritual, spiritual, it approaches the soundless. Thus they can be the master of the enemy's fate."

SAWYER

In the Warring States period, cities found themselves compelled to organize their entire populaces to survive assaults and sieges. The *Mo-tzu*, which focused on defensive warfare in consonance with Mo-tzu's doctrines, outlines tactics for repelling attacks and thwarting mining and incendiary measures and provides numerous organizational measures intended to maintain security under duress. The late *Wei Liao-tzu* even includes a chapter titled "Tactical Balance of Power in Defense" that specifies the manpower required to man the walls. However, it opens by outlining the steps that should be taken to defend the city in general, including the imposition of a relatively circumscribed scorched earth policy:

> In general, when the defenders go forth, if they do not [occupy] the outer walls of the cities nor the borderlands and when they retreat do not [establish] watchtowers and barricades for the purpose of defensive warfare, they do not excel [at defense]. The valiant heroes and brave stalwarts, sturdy armor and sharp weapons, powerful crossbows and strong arrows should all be within the outer walls, all [the grain stored outside] in the earthen cellars and granaries collected, and the buildings [outside the outer walls] broken down and brought into the fortifications. This will force the attackers to expend ten or a hundred times the energy, while the defenders will not expend half theirs. Enemy aggressors will thus be greatly harmed, yet generals through the ages have not known this.

The core of Li Ch'üan's concerns can be found in a passage contained in the *Shang-chün Shu*, the work attributed to the "realist" reformer Shang Yang who had been instrumental in revising Ch'in's laws and establishing bold new policies in the middle fourth century BCE. Shang's efforts not only strengthened Ch'in's military and enabled the state to prosper, but also created the foundation for the expansionist thrust that eventually saw it conquer the remaining states and unify the empire. In a section generally known as "Troops in Defense" (兵 守), he asserts:

> The Tao of defense is to fully exhaust your strength. Stalwart men should comprise one army, robust women another army, and the old and weak among the men and women another. They are termed the "Three Armies."
> Have the army of stalwart men, with abundant provisions and sharp weapons, deploy to await the enemy. The army of robust women should deploy along the ramparts with abundant provisions and await orders. When the "guest" arrives, they should [extemporaneously] create alleys and obstacles of

earth and dig out trenches and pits. They should also remove the beams from houses and take apart the houses [located on the exterior], moving whatever is possible within the city and burning whatever cannot be moved so as to prevent the guest from employing these materials to augment their assault preparations.

The army of old and weak should take charge of herding the oxen, horses, sheep, and swine, and they should gather whatever grass and water can be eaten to feed them (in the city) and thereby provide for the sturdy men and women. Be careful not to allow any of the Three Armies to encounter each other because if the stalwart men pass the army of robust women, the men will be concerned for the women, and the licentious will engage in intrigue, resulting in the state being lost. Moreover, when they are happy [at being together], they will fear that troublesome matters might arise, and the men [will not be inclined] to fight.

If the stalwart men and robust women should encounter the army of the old and weak, the aged will cause the stalwart to feel grief, and the weak will cause the strong to feel pity. When grief and pity affect the heart, courageous people become anxious, and the fearful will not fight. Thus it is said that one must ensure that the Three Armies do not encounter each other. This is the Tao for fully exhausting one's strength.

Measures for urban defense had begun to evolve in the Spring and Autumn period when cities became deliberately chosen objectives, prompting Sun-tzu's admonition to avoid assaulting fortified population centers. Accordingly, discussions of basic issues and tactical methods for both attack and defense are found scattered throughout the classic military writings. However, it is in the *Wei Liao-tzu*, compiled after at least three centuries of experience in sieges and assaults, that the most thorough analyses appear. Defense is the focus of "Tactical Balance of Power in Defense," a chapter already mentioned at the start of the commentary:

The defenders should not neglect the strategic points. The rule for defending a city wall is that for every *chang* [ten feet] you should employ ten men to defend it, artisans and cooks not being included. Those who go out [to fight] do not defend the city; those that defend the city do not go out [to fight]. One man [on defense] can oppose ten men [besieging them]; ten men can oppose a hundred men; a hundred men can oppose a thousand men; a thousand men can oppose ten thousand men. Thus constructing [a city's] interior and exterior walls by accumulating loose soil [and tamping it down] does not wantonly expend the strength of the people, for it truly is for defense.

If a wall is a thousand *chang*, then ten thousand men should defend it. The moats should be deep and wide, the walls solid and thick, the soldiers and people prepared, firewood and foodstuffs provided, the crossbows stout and arrows strong, the spears and halberds well suited. This is the method for making defense solid.

If the attackers are not less than a mass of at least a hundred thousand, while [the defenders] have an army outside that will certainly come to the rescue, it is a city that must be defended. If there is no external army to inevitably rescue them, then it isn't a city that must be defended.

Now, if the walls are solid and rescue certain, then even stupid men and ignorant women will all, without exception, protect the walls, exhausting their resources and blood for them. For a city to withstand a siege for a year, the [strength of] the defenders should exceed that of the attackers, and the [strength of] the rescue force exceed that of the defenders.

A paired chapter titled "Tactical Balance of Power in Attack," although pointedly intended to discuss the concerns of aggressors, indirectly illuminates the behavior and measures that will ensure a successful defense or fate a city to destruction:

If you occupy [the terrain around] a city or town and sever the various roads about it, follow up by attacking the city itself. If the enemy's generals and armies are unable to believe in each other, the officers and troops unable to be in harmony, and there are those who are unaffected by punishments, we will defeat them. Before the rescue party has arrived, the city will have already surrendered.

If fords and bridges have not yet been constructed, strategic barriers not yet repaired, dangerous points in the city walls not yet fortified, and the iron caltrops not yet set out, then even though they have fortifications, they do not have any defense!

If the troops from distant forts have not yet entered [the city] and the border guards and forces in other states have not yet returned, then even though they have men, they do not have any men! If the six domesticated animals have not yet been herded in, the five grains not yet harvested, their wealth and essential materials for use not yet collected, then even though they have resources, they do not have any resources! Now, when a city is empty and void and its resources are exhausted, we should take advantage of this vacuity to attack them.

Another section, "Military Instructions, II," outlines some basic criteria for deciding whether a city can or should be attacked that coincidentally indicate what might be considered vulnerabilities: "When the general is light, the fortifications low, and the people's minds unstable, they can be attacked. If the general is weighty and the fortifications are high, but the masses are afraid, they can be encircled." Even if the inhabitants are initially unified, they can be psychologically weakened:

In general, whenever you encircle someone, you must provide them with a prospect for some minor advantage, causing them to become weaker day by day. Then the defenders will be forced to reduce their rations until they have nothing to eat. When their masses fight with each other at night, they are terrified, and if they avoid their work, they have become disaffected. If they just wait for others to come and rescue them and are tense when the time for battle arrives, they have all lost their will and are dispirited. Dispirit defeats an army, distorted plans defeat a state.

Aquatic attacks often relied upon complete encirclement and flooding the city in depth, precluding any opportunity to flee.

Finally, the first paragraph concludes with a derivative version of Sun-tzu's statement from "Military Disposition" that "one who cannot be victorious assumes a defensive posture, one who can be victorious attacks. In these circumstances by assuming a defensive posture, strength will be more than adequate whereas in offensive actions it would be inadequate." The premise for these measures just precedes them in the *Art of War*: "Being unconquerable lies with yourself, being conquerable lies with the enemy. Thus one who excels in warfare is able to make himself unconquerable but cannot necessarily cause the enemy to be conquerable."

Sun-tzu's concept of conquerable and unconquerable has occasioned considerable confusing commentary. However, Li Ch'üan penetrates the essential meaning with a commentary that translates the abstract into concrete methods:

> One who excels in employing the army makes his walls thick when defending and multiplies his equipment, chariots, and provisions. He excels at instructing and training. When he assaults a city, he employs attack chariots, mobile protective shields, cloud ladders, earthen (overlook) mounds, and tunnels. When he deploys [in the field], he keeps rivers and marshes on the left and mounds and hillocks on the right. He keeps isolated terrain behind and orients toward vacuity, he releases the doubtful and strikes the gaps. Those who excel at warfare divide into separate contingents for pincer attacks and have their strategic power interconnected so that the head and tail respond to each other and they cannot be conquered.

The responsiveness of the head and tail are found in an *Art of War* passage that states: "One who excels at employing the army may be compared to the *shuai-jan* [snake]. The *shuai-jan* is found on Mt. Ch'ang. It you strike its head, the tail will respond; if you strike its tail, the head will respond. If you strike the middle, both the head and tail will react."

MINOR JOTTINGS:

Incendiary and aquatic warfare, including the methods and materials found in the *T'ai-pai Yin-ching*, are discussed in my *Fire and Water: Incendiary and Aquatic Warfare in China*. Incendiary techniques, being the easiest to implement yet highly effective, were more commonly undertaken than the laborious diversion and encirclement efforts required to flood a target.

23

行 人

"ROVING AGENTS"

If the ruler selects a day to ascend the altar and appoint a commanding general; has the weapons and armor put into good order; the troops venture forth to destroy the enemy's state, defeat the enemy's army, kill the enemy's general, and take their people prisoner; transports provisions out ten thousand *li*; and penetrates the enemy's borders, yet does not know the enemy's true situation, this is the commanding general's error.

The enemy's true situation cannot be discerned among the stars and constellations, nor sought from ghosts and spirits, nor acquired through divination or prognostication, but can be sought among men. In antiquity, when the Shang arose, Yi Yin was a cook in the Hsia; when the Chou arose, the T'ai Kung was a fisherman in the Shang; when the Ch'in established imperial rule, Li Ssu was a hunter in Shandong; when Han Kao-tsu became king, Han Hsin was an exiled soldier from Ch'u; and when Ts'ao

Ts'ao found him, Hsün Yü was Yüan Shao's cast off minister. Ssu-ma T'an became emperor of Chin because Chia Ch'ung had been entrusted with government in Wei, while Wei itself arose because Ts'ui Hao had made Chin his home. Through employing these men, seven rulers became emperors over All under Heaven.

Whenever worthy men flee a state, it must be because sycophantic ministers control the ruler's authority. The true measure of things is then lost; the ruler's assistants form cliques; men of little merit monopolize power; and scoundrels usurp the authority of state. For example, T'ui Yi promiscuously served King Chieh of the Hsia, Ch'ung Hou flattered Chieh of the Shang, and Yu Shih befuddled Chin. Shih Tu assisted the Yu Yü, Ku Kung monopolized power among the Huan Tou, and Ch'eng Chün exercised authority among the San Miao. Thus it is said that when its three benevolent advisers departed, the Shang became a wasteland, and when the two elders gave their allegiance to the Chou, it became glorious. When Wu Tzu-hsü died, the state of Wu was lost. Fan Li lived and Yüeh became hegemon, Wu Ku entered the border and Ch'in was delighted, and [general] Yüeh Yi departed and Yen was terrified.

When a general succeeds in securing the enemy's people, entrusts them with responsibility, and ferrets out the enemy's true situation, what worry will there be that he might not be victorious? Thus it is said that if you gather in their stalwarts, the enemy's state will be overturned; if you snare their valiants, the enemy's state will be empty. Truly, through stones from other mountains you can polish your own jade.

Now, there are two employments for roving agents [hsing-jen]. First, we can capitalize upon the men dispatched by the enemy to observe our defects by offering them higher ranks and making their salaries more generous. Thereafter, investigate their words and compare them with actuality. If they prove accurate, you can then employ them; if specious, you can execute them. Employ them as "local guides."

Second, have our roving agents observe the enemy's ruler and ministers, attendants, and officials that control affairs, noting who among them are worthy, who stupid. Among the ruler's intimates both inside and outside the palace, who is covetous, who incorruptible? Among his attendants and diplomatic personnel, who are perfected men, who menial men? Once we have acquired this knowledge, we can proceed to achieve our purpose.

Among those serving in the Three Armies, none are more important than roving agents. Among secrets within the Three Armies, none are more secret than [the affairs of] roving agents. When clandestine plots for employing roving agents have not yet been set into motion, all those who leak them as well as everyone they inform should be executed. On the day action is initiated, destroy the documents, burn the drafts, silence their mouths, and do not allow internal plans to leak out. Be like birds of prey invisibly entering heavy forests or fish diving into deep pools without any trace. Remember that despite his surpassing visual acuity, Li Lou couldn't discern the shape of things when he bent his head, and despite his acute hearing, Shih Kuang couldn't hear a sound when he tilted his ear downward. Subtle, subtle, just like a swirl of fine dust arising. How can drunken and sated generals who contend with force and lightly engage in battle manage to discern the affairs of roving agents?

SAWYER

In "Roving Agents" Li Ch'üan revived the old term of *hsing-jen*, a title that had designated a Chou dynasty official entrusted with political reconnaissance missions. The first two paragraphs essentially replicate Sun-tzu's behest to rely solely upon the human realm (already cited in the *T'ai-pai Yin-ching*'s first chapter) and repeat his justification for employing spies, which, although primarily economic, encompassed the ruthless pursuit of noncombat objectives such as balking plans and thwarting alliances. (As expressed in the *Art of War*, prolonged warfare is condemned because it enervates the state and thus tempts others to undertake predatory actions, rather than because casualties are being suffered.)

167

However, in addition to the heavy sustainment burdens that ongoing campaigns impose, some seven families said by Sun-tzu to have been necessary to support each fighter, parsimoniousness can prolong the conflict and thus cause unconscionable loss: "Armies remain locked in a standoff for years to fight for victory on a single day, yet [generals] begrudge bestowing ranks and emoluments of one hundred pieces of gold and therefore do not know the enemy's situation. This is the ultimate inhumanity. Such a person is not a general for the people, an assistant for a ruler, or the arbiter of victory."

The *Art of War*, historically the first work to ponder the theory and nature of spycraft, identifies five types of agent and defines them by their activities and objectives: "There are five types of spies to be employed: local spies, internal spies, turned spies [double agents], dead [expendable] spies, and living spies. For local spies, employ people from the local district; for internal spies, employ their people who hold government positions; for double agents, employ the enemy's spies; and expendable spies are employed to spread disinformation outside the state. Provide our [expendable] spies [with false information] and have them leak it to enemy agents. Living spies return with their reports."

Li simplified them considerably by envisioning a need for just two types of operatives, doubled agents and spies that would be employed in foreign states to gain detailed knowledge of the enemy's staff and court personalities in preparation for mounting subversive actions. The *Art of War* summarily discusses the means for acquiring "turned agents" as well as their importance and objectives: "You must search for enemy agents who have come to spy on us. Tempt them with profits, instruct and retain them. Thus double agents can be obtained and employed. Through knowledge gained from them, you can recruit both local and internal spies. Through knowledge gained from them, the expendable spy can spread his falsehoods and can be used to misinform the enemy. Through knowledge gained from them, our living spies can be employed as times require." Clearly the double agent was a lynchpin in the information war that had already been emerging because Sun-tzu added the comment that "the ruler must know these five aspects of espionage work. This knowledge inevitably depends on turned spies; therefore, you must be generous to double agents."

Being comparable to Sun-tzu's "living spies," Li's ordinary agents were dispatched to foreign states on information-gathering missions similar to those defined in the Art of War: "In general, as for the armies you want to strike, the cities you want to attack, and the men you want to assassinate, you must first know the names of the defensive commander, his assistants, staff, door guards, and attendants. You must have our spies search out and learn them all." Since a focal task would be identifying disaffected and otherwise corruptible people in positions of power or influence, the intent was to then employ them for subversive purposes, no doubt (although unstated) as internal spies. (In his Art of War commentary, Li particularly advises "relying upon enemy personnel who have lost their posts.")

Although unmentioned by Li Ch'üan, Sun-tzu had stressed that anyone who hoped to successfully employ spies must be a paragon of wisdom and uprightness. In addition, just as Li Ch'üan in "The Army's Form," Sun-tzu also emphasized the need for secrecy in a paragraph that "Roving Agents" essentially adopts: "Thus of all the Three Armies' affairs, no relationship is closer than with spies; no rewards are more generous than those given to spies, no affairs are more secret than those pertaining to spies. If before the mission has begun it has already been exposed, the spy and those he informed should all be put to death."

However, as "Roving Agents" points out, information should not be acquired solely through clandestine measures. Defectors, particularly those who voluntarily changed allegiance rather than having been induced to waver through bribes or coercion, historically provided secret information and undertook vital strategic and advisory functions. Their numbers most famously include Yi Yin and the T'ai Kung, both of whom are cited in the Art of War and T'ai-pai Yin-ching because their guidance proved instrumental in the Shang's and Chou's efforts to overthrow the established powers and thereby found new dynasties. These functions apart, (as already seen) acquiring talented personnel from the enemy and gathering in their people were primary objectives in the quest to achieve victory.

MINOR JOTTINGS:

The theory and techniques of spycraft evolved considerably over the centuries from Sun-tzu's *Art of War* and early historic practices. The number of agents entrusted with distinctive missions and the techniques to be employed in the field and for counterintelligence work all multiplied, resulting in a copious body of theoretical material and numerous case studies. (For an extended discussion, see our *Tao of Spycraft*.)

24

鑒　才

"MIRRORING TALENT"

The classics state that men are born through encompassing original *ch'i* and are completed through *yin* and *yang*. Purity, harmony, tranquility, and placidity are [aspects of] original *ch'i*; penetration, clarity, refinement (*chün*), and heroism are [aspects of] *yin* and *yang*. The pure and harmonious do not understand situational change, the penetrating and enlightened do not comprehend the Tao's subtle depths.

Men who are flexible, orderly, tranquil, and compassionate suffer from indecisiveness so they are effective in well regulated affairs but have difficulty responding to fluctuating situations. The strong, fierce, hard, and courageous suffer from suspiciousness and jealousy so they can overcome [momentary] challenges but lack resilience. The truthful, good, fearful, and cautious tend to hesitate and be doubtful so they take pleasure in accomplishments but have difficulty initiating plans. The unblemished, scrupulous, and pure tend to be confounded by affairs so they can undertake organized matters but are not able to penetrate changes. The secretive, morose, contemplative, and tranquil become lost in reflection and pondering so they can engage in deep planning but find it difficult to respond to rapidly changing circumstances.

Superiority in penetrating enlightenment is termed *ying* (brilliant 英), courage and strength that surpass other men is termed *hsiung* (heroic 雄). The brilliant are wise, the heroic strong. The brilliant cannot be decisive and daring, the heroic cannot be wise and make strategic plans. Thus when the brilliant acquire the [characteristics of] the heroic they can implement affairs, when the heroic acquire the [characteristics of] the brilliant they can realize achievements.

By nature men fall into eight different types: benevolent, righteous, loyal, trustworthy, wise, courageous, greedy, and stupid. The benevolent love to bespread [beneficence], the righteous love intimacy, the loyal like straightforwardness, the trustworthy like to preserve, the wise like to plan, the courageous like to be decisive, the greedy love to take, and the stupid love to boast.

When rulers embrace benevolence and righteousness All under Heaven will be attracted. When they incline to loyalty and good faith [the inhabitants] of the four seas will become honored guests; when they incline to wisdom and courage the feudal lords will become their subjects, but when they combine greed and stupidity they will be governed by others.

The benevolent and righteous can plan horizontal alliances, the wise and courageous can plan vertical alliances. Those who plan horizontal alliances become kings, those who plan vertical ones become hegemons. The Tao of hegemons and kings does not lie in the interstice of strong troops and courageous officers but in the realm of benevolence, righteousness, wisdom, and courage. However, these are partial talents, not the basis for speaking about great generals. But someone who can be flexible and hard, contract and expand, be brilliant (*ying*) and courageous, heroic (*hsiung*) and make plans, round and able to revolve, circular without starting points, fully knowledgeable about the myriad things and able to cause them to be unified throughout the realm is termed a penetrating talent and can be a great general.

Thus it is said that generals are the support of the state. When the supporters [have] all encompassing talent the state will be strong, when the supporters are marked by deficiencies the state will be weak. They are referred to as the people's "masters of fate," rulers of the state's security and endangerment, so they must be investigated.

When a perspicacious ruler selects men he examines their talent to see if it is penetrating and complete; he scrutinizes their appearance to see if it is generous and noble; he investigates their minds to see if they are upright and bright. He dwells on high and looks out far, he leisurely sees and expansively listens. He makes his appearance spiritual and concentrates his vital spirit, becoming like the heights of a lofty mountain that cannot be reached or the depths of a spring that cannot be fathomed. Thereafter he investigates their worthiness and stupidity through words and phrases and determines their wisdom and courage by entrusting them with affairs, only after which he can employ them.

Now he selects the sagacious through the Tao, the worthy through Virtue, the wise through plans, the courageous through strength, the greedy though profit, the villainous through fissures, and the stupid through endangerment. He agrees with them in affairs to examine their Tao, disagrees with them in affairs to observe their Virtue. When tactical circumstances change he observes their plans, when [they are engaged in] attacking and seizing he observes their courage. When they are entrusted with material goods he observes how they manage their profits, when responsible for inner palace affairs he observes their deficiencies, and when they are in frightening circumstances he observes [how they handle] security and endangerment.

Thus it is said that if you want to fathom their coming, look at their going; if you want to know their history, investigate the present. Those who investigate before they entrust people with responsibility flourish, those who entrust people with responsibility before investigating perish. In antiquity, when Shih Yü sold goods in Chin the ruler investigated and employed him to gain victory over Ch'u. When Yi Yin sold goods in the Shang, King T'ang examined and employed him to depose Chieh. [Finding the] wise and capable is not a question of distance or nearness. Straightened and perverse circumstances do not prevent the benevolent from displaying their Virtue nor do wise officers fail to manifest their achievements because the times are not conducive. Nearly perishing does not prevent [true] kings from establishing their righteousness nor do strong enemies prevent hegemons from keeping misfortune at bay.

When enlightened rulers employ men they do not lose the capable, when upright officers raise the worthy they will not fail to always perform effectively. Someone without the wisdom of a myriad cannot dwell atop a myriad. Thus it is said that if someone does not know military affairs but undertakes to govern them the officers will be befuddled, if he does not know the authority of the three armies but takes control of them military affairs will be thrown into doubt. When the three armies are confused and doubtful it will prompt the other feudal lords to initiate predatory actions.

When this has been achieved the ruler will not be king in name alone nor ministers speciously ennobled. This is what is meant by the Tao of rulers who know how to employ subordinates and subordinates having techniques to serve their rulers.

SAWYER:

"Chien Ts'ai" accords with the thrust of "Numerous Methods for Probing the Mind," the key difference being that though the latter focuses upon aggressively interviewing people and verbally controlling them through their penchants whereas "Mirroring Talent" is concerned with evaluating men and their abilities. (As discussed in the introduction, another chapter in this same vein, "Scrutinizing Men," attempts to correlate appearance with character and capability.)

By Li Ch'üan's era men had long been conscious that character might be discerned and intent fathomed by observing attitude and behavior. Furthermore, they had realized that even though people maintained deliberate facades and tried to disguise their true nature, stimulating them in specific ways could prompt responses that would reveal their true personality as well as their flaws and virtues. Thus a number of tests evolved, some commonly known, others articulated only in arcane writings such as the *Kuei Ku-tzu* (previously mentioned in "Techniques for Probing the Mind") or preserved in remnant texts including the *Yi Chou-shu* (*Remnant Books of the Chou*). Highly desirable combinations of traits and capabilities were also recognized and the dangers of even the most praiseworthy virtues pondered, many of the conclusions then being codified in the *Six Secret Teachings* and in passages scattered among the other classic military writings.

"Generals of Wisdom and Strategy" having already examined the traits required for successful generalship and outlined the implications of significant character flaws, a couple of historical approaches to actively testing men might prove illustrative. "Six Preservations" in the *Six Secret Teachings* contains the best known measures for actively evaluating other people:

> King Wen asked: "What are the six preservations ?"
>
> The T'ai Kung replied: "The first is called benevolence, the second righteousness, the third loyalty, the fourth trust (good faith), the fifth courage, and the sixth planning. These are referred to as the six preservations."
>
> King Wen asked: "How does one go about carefully selecting men using the six preservations ?"
>
> The T'ai Kung responded: "Make them rich and observe whether they do not commit offenses. Give them rank and observe whether they do not become arrogant. Entrust them with responsibility and see whether they will not change. Employ them and see whether they will not conceal anything. Endanger them and see whether they are not afraid. Entrust them with the management of affairs and see whether they are not perplexed.

If you make them rich but they do not commit offenses they are benevolent. If you give them rank and they do not grow arrogant they are righteous. If you entrust them with office and they do not change, they are loyal. If you employ them and they do not conceal anything they are trustworthy. If you put them in danger and they are not afraid they are courageous. If you give them the management of affairs and they are not perplexed they are capable of making plans.

A lengthy chapter common to the *Yi Chou-shu* and *Ta Tai Li-chi* known as "The Offices of King Wen" preserves even more extensive material. A work that probably attained final form in the third century BCE, it purportedly records a lecture delivered by King Wen, one of the Chou Dynasty's progenitors, to the T'ai Kung on the difficult task of evaluating, selecting, and employing men. Even though the king admits that "the people have *yin* and *yang* aspects and there are many who conceal their emotions, who adorn themselves with artifice in order to seek fame," he steadfastly believes that character can be fathomed, that emotions and true personality cannot be concealed and he therefore provides a sophisticated analysis of character types, associated facades, and potential for government service. The lecture not only integrates a wealth of detail but also integrates and exploits Warring States period knowledge of human tendencies, the latter assessed against those of an ideal figure. The king even outlines a number of psychological principles that make the process possible including consistency of behavior.

The chapter thus constitutes a complete and extensive analytical guidebook for classifying personality and evaluating ability, as well as an intrinsic source book on character typology. Although its length precludes replicating it here, the following abstracts are particularly illustrative and may be taken as representative of the state of character analysis prior to Li Ch'üan's own formulation.

King Wen said: "T'ai-shih, you must be cautious and ponder deeply, observe the affairs of the people, investigate and measure their emotions and artifices, make changes in official positions to see their ability to [govern] the people, and array them by their talents and skills. You must be cautious ! How can you be careful about those that are not of the right ability ?

There are seven categories of ability; each category has nine employments; and each employment has six indications. The first is observe his sincerity; the second is test his intentions; the third is look within; the fourth is observe his appearance; the fifth is observe his hidden aspects; the six is estimate his virtue."

· · · · · ·

Test him to observe his trustworthiness. Give him some cues to observe his wisdom. Show him hardship in order to observe his courage. Annoy him with small matters in order to see how he handles it. Immerse him in profit in order to observe whether he isn't greedy. Immerse him in pleasure to observe whether he doesn't become dissolute. Make him happy with things to observe whether he doesn't become frivolous.

Make him angry in order to observe his gravity. Make him drunk in order to observe if he does not violate propriet. Indulge him in order to observe the mainstays of his character. Keep him at a distance in order to see if he is not disloyal. Keep him nearby in order to see if he doesn't become too familiar. Sound out his intentions in order to observe his emotions. Try his behavior in order to observe his sincerity. Revisit his minor words to observe his truthfulness. Surreptitiously investigate his behavior in order to observe if it is complete.

Unfortunately, it remains unclear how extensively these techniques were employed in either the civil or martial realms across China's many centuries.

25

授 鉞

"BESTOWING THE YÜEH [AX]"

The [*Six Secret Teachings*] states that when the state suffers military activities out on the border, the Son of Heaven should dwell in the Main Hall, summon the general, and charge him as follows: "Being without Virtue I mistakenly accepted the indications of Heaven [and ascended the throne], resulting in invaders encroaching upon our border, causing chaos, attacking, and plundering. I forget to eat until the day is nearly over and am worried when I try to sleep. I would therefore trouble your martial spirit to lead the army forth in response."

The general bows twice and receives his mandate, after which [the ruler] orders the grand scribe to perform divination. Thereafter, he observes a vegetarian regime for three days and then at the *T'ai Miao* [Grand Ancestral Temple] has the Grand Scribe heat the sacred tortoise shell to divine [an auspicious day] for handing over the *fu* and *yueh* axes.

179

The ruler enters the *T'ai Miao* and stands facing west. The ruler personally grasps the great *yüeh* ax in order to bestow it upon the general and says: "From this to Heaven above will be controlled by the general of the army." Then again grasping the *fu* ax by the handle, he gives it to the general, saying, "From this to the springs below will be controlled by the general of the army."

After the general has received his mandate, he kneels and replies: "I have heard that a state cannot follow external dictates and an army [in the field] cannot follow internal governance. Someone of two minds cannot properly serve his ruler, someone with doubtful intentions cannot respond to the enemy. I have already received the mandate and taken control of the awesomeness of the *fu* and *yüeh* axes. I do not dare return alive. I request that you grant complete and sole command to me. If you do not permit this, I dare not accept the generalship." The king then grants it, and the general formally takes his leave and goes forth [with the army].

When the Three Armies are engaged in military affairs, commands from the ruler are not obeyed but instead all proceed from the commanding general. When [the commanding general] goes forth, approaches the enemy, and engages in decisive battle, he is not of two minds. In this way there is no Heaven above, no Earth below, no orders from the ruler in the middle, and no enemies to the side. For this reason the wise make plans for him, the courageous fight for him. Their spirit soars to the blue clouds, they are swift like galloping steeds. Even before the blades clash, the enemy surrenders submissively.

War is won outside [the state], but merit is established within it. [The campaign having concluded], the commanding general dons the white garb [of mourning], dwells apart, and beseeches the ruler [to rescind his authority]. The ruler then orders him to relinquish it.

SAWYER

As noted in the introduction, this chapter outlines the essentials of a ceremony designed to formally bestow military authority upon the commanding general and thereby empower him not just with responsibility but also the requisite awesomeness. ("The Government Executes the Strong" previously discussed measures for augmenting it as well.) It basically adopts the text of a dedicated chapter found in the *Six Secret Teachings* and therefore dates back to the middle to late Warring States period. However, even though the usual admonitions about the general's proper behavior found therein are dispersed throughout the *T'ai-pai Yin-ching*, especially "Troops," Li Ch'üan left them out here:

> When you see a vacuity in the enemy, you should advance; when you see substance, you should halt. Do not assume that the Three Armies are large and treat the enemy lightly. Do not commit yourself to die just because you have received a heavy responsibility. Do not, because you are honored, regard other men as lowly. Do not rely upon yourself alone and contravene the masses. Do not take verbal facility to be a sign of certainty. When the officers have not yet been seated, do not sit. When the officers have not yet eaten, do not eat. You should share heat and cold with them. If you behave in this way, the officers and masses will certainly exhaust their strength in fighting to the death.

The conclusion also differs slightly because "Appointing the General" states that "officials are promoted and receive the highest rewards; the hundred surnames rejoice; and the general is blameless. For this reason the winds and rains will be seasonable; the five grains will grow abundantly; and the altars of state will be secure and peaceful."

The formal granting and rescinding of martial authority well accorded not just with the necessities of political and military power but also the emphasis found in the *Ssu-ma Fa* that the two realms — the martial (*wu*) and civil (*wen*) — are fundamentally distinct:

> In antiquity the form and spirit governing civilian affairs would not be found in the military realm; those appropriate to

the military realm would not be found in the civilian sphere. If the form and spirit [appropriate to the] military realm enter the civilian sphere, the Virtue of the people will decline. When the form and spirit [appropriate to the] civilian sphere enter the military realm, then the Virtue of the people will weaken. In the civilian sphere, words are cultivated and speech languid. In court one is respectful and courteous and cultivates himself to serve others. Unsummoned, he does not step forth; unquestioned, he does not speak. It is difficult to advance but easy to withdraw.

In the military realm, one speaks directly and stands firm. When deployed in formation, one focuses on duty and acts decisively. Those wearing battle armor do not bow; those in war chariots need not observe the forms of propriety [*li* 禮]; those manning fortifications do not scurry. In times of danger, one does not pay attention to seniority. Thus the civilian forms of behavior [*li*] and military standards [*fa* 法] are like inside and outside; the civil and martial are like left and right.

Victory in military campaigns not only spawned euphoria and tilted prevailing values toward the martial but also nurtured generals powerful enough to pose potential challenges to the political authorities, however sanctioned or perverse the latter might be. Accordingly, the *Three Strategies of Huang-shih Kung* noted in its "Middle Strategy" that a return to "normalcy" must be effected:

When the soaring birds have all been slain, then good bows are stored away. When enemy states have been extinguished, ministers in charge of planning are lost. Here "lost" doesn't mean they lose their lives, but that [the ruler] has taken away their awesomeness and removed their authority. He enfeoffs them in court at the highest ranks of his subordinates in order to manifest their merit. He presents them with excellent states in the central region in order to enrich their families and bestows beautiful women and valuable treasures upon them in order to please their hearts.

Now, once the masses have been brought together, they cannot be hastily separated. Once the awesomeness of authority has been granted, it cannot be suddenly shifted. Returning the forces and disbanding the armies are critical stages in preservation and loss. Thus weakening [the commanding general] through appointment to new positions, taking [his authority] by granting him a state, is referred to as a hegemon's strategy.

The general's donning of white garb—white being the color of mourning in traditional China—reflects the *Tao Te Ching*'s view that warfare is a sorrowful affair. According to the last lines of "Superlative Weapons," parts of which have already been encountered:

> Victories achieved are not glorified,
> For glorifying them is to take pleasure in killing men.
> One who takes pleasure in killing men
> Cannot achieve his ambitions under Heaven.
> Auspicious affairs esteem the left,
> Inauspicious affairs esteem the right.
> Subordinate generals occupy the left,
> Commanding generals the right.
> This states that one treats military affairs as rites of mourning.
> After killing masses of the enemy's men,
> Weep for them with grief and sorrow.
> After being victorious in battle,
> Implement the rites of mourning.

Finally, the need for generals to be free from political interference in the midst of battlefield operations, already noted in earlier *T'ai-pai Yin-ching* chapters, was first articulated in the *Art of War* when it observed that "there are three ways by which an army is put into difficulty by a ruler":

He does not know that the Three Armies should not advance but instructs them to advance, or does not know that the Three Armies should not withdraw and orders them to retreat. This is termed "entangling the army."

He does not understand the Three Armies' military affairs but directs them in the same way as his civil administration. Then the officers will become confused.

He does not understand the Three Armies' tactical balance of power but undertakes responsibility for command. Then the officers will be doubtful.

No doubt Sun-tzu's motives were multiple, ranging from concern over the ruler's ignorance of military matters through the slowness and therefore irrelevance of communications. Accordingly he concluded: "When the Three Armies are already confused and doubtful, the danger of the feudal lords taking advantage of the situation arises. This is referred to as 'a disordered army drawing another on to victory.'" Conversely, "Those whose generals are capable and not interfered with by the ruler will be victorious." All the classic military writings subsequently embraced this need for professional independence, with statements such as "The commanding general is not governed by Heaven above, controlled by Earth below, or governed by men in the middle," found in the *Wei Liao-tzu*'s "Military Discussions."

MINOR JOTTINGS:

A variant but unlikely interpretation of the last line holds that it means the general removes the army thirty *li* and then petitions for release from command.

SUGGESTIONS FOR FURTHER READING

The best overview of T'ang historical developments remains *The Cambridge History of China: Sui and T'ang China, 589–906*, edited by Denis Twitchett. T'ang military history has primarily been studied by David Graff, whose volume *Medieval Chinese Warfare, 300–900* provides the sole introduction to events in English. Several of his articles also merit consulting: "The Sword and the Brush: Military Specialization and Career Patterns in Tang China, 618–907," *War and Society* 18.2 (October 2000), pp. 9–21; "Li Jing's Antecedents: Continuity and Change in the Pragmatics of Medieval Chinese Warfare," *Early Medieval China* 13–14:1 (2007), pp. 81–97; "Strategy and Contingency in the Tang Defeat of the Eastern Turks, 629–30" in *Warfare in Inner Asian History (500–1800)*, edited by Nicola Di Cosmo; and "Narrative Maneuvers: The Representation of Battle in Tang Historical Writings" in *Military Culture in Imperial China*, again edited by Nicola Di Cosmo.

For a general discussion of the classic and later military texts in China see Sawyer, "Military Writings" in *A Military History of China*, edited by David A. Graff and Robin Higham. Sun-tzu's *Art of War* has been translated several times over the past century by people with varying expertise; suggested versions include either General Griffith's *Art of War* or my own for military interpretations, especially my single volume edition which contains an extensive historical introduction; Roger Ames's, *The Art of Warfare*, for a more philosophical orientation; and Victor Mair's for the most recent redaction.

The *Sun Pin Ping-fa* enjoys two translations, my own under the title of *Sun Pin Military Methods* and Roger Ames and D. C. Lau's, *Sun Bin: The Art of Warfare*.

The *Wu-tzu* appears in my *Seven Military Classics of Ancient China* as well as Griffith's *Art of War*.

Most of the other classic military writings — the *Ssu-ma Fa, Six Secret Teachings, Wei Liao-tzu,* and *Three Strategies of Huang-shih Kung* — exist only in my translations and may all be found in my *Seven Military Classics of Ancient China*.

The *Tao Te Ching* has been rendered into English dozens of times, obviating any need for a recommendation apart from noting that my translation under the title *The Tao of War: The Martial Tao Te Ching* is the only one to interpret it as a military work. Fortunately the *Huai-nan Tzu* can now be found in a translation by John S. Major and his associates, *The Huainanzi: A Guide to the Theory and Practice of Government in Early Han China*. J. L. L. Duyvendak's nearly century-old rendition of the *Shang-chün Shu* remains available under the title of *The Book of Lord Shang*, and John Knoblock has provided a complete version of Hsün-tzu, *Xunzi: A Translation and Study of the Complete Works*.

Translations of the historical works that Li Ch'üan consulted include James Legge's classic *Tso Chuan* (with selections also being provided by Burton Watson in a dedicated volume) and numerous chapters from the *Shih Chi* by both Watson and a group of scholars under the general editorship of William Nienhauser, Jr.

The thorny subject of martial prognostication has been discussed in several of my publications, including "Paradoxical

Coexistence of Prognostication and Warfare" (*Sino-Platonic Papers* #157) and "Martial Prognostication" in *Military Culture in Imperial China*, edited by Nicola Di Cosmo. (Those interested in another example from the Chinese divinatory tradition may consult our translation of the most popular Chinese prognosticatory manual, itself an alternative to the *Yi Ching*, titled the *Ling Ch'i Ching: A Classic Chinese Oracle*.)

Finally, discussions of military matters raised in the commentaries may be found in several of my books, including the *Tao of Spycraft*, *Tao of Deception*, and *Ancient Chinese Warfare* as well as an article on courage and spirit, "Martial Qi in China: Courage and Spirit in Thought and Military Practice," *Journal of Military and Strategic Studies*, Winter 2008/2009, available at www.jmss.org.

INDEX TO CRUCIAL CONCEPTS AND TACTICAL PRINCIPLES IN THE TEXT OF THE *T'AI-PAI YIN-CHING*

(ALL REFERENCES ARE TO CHAPTER NUMBERS)

Printed in Great Britain
by Amazon